UNODA

United Nations Office for
Disarmament Affairs

UNODA Occasional Papers

No. 29, October 2016

Bringing Democracy to Disarmament

A Historical Perspective on the Special Sessions of the General Assembly Devoted to Disarmament

by Randy J. Rydell, PhD

United Nations

The United Nations Office for Disarmament Affairs (UNODA) Occasional Papers are a series of ad hoc publications featuring, in edited form, papers or statements made at meetings, symposiums, seminars, workshops or lectures that deal with topical issues in the field of arms limitation, disarmament and international security. They are intended primarily for those concerned with these matters in Government, civil society and in the academic community.

The views expressed in this publication are those of the author and do not necessarily reflect those of the United Nations or its Member States.

Material in UNODA Occasional Papers may be reprinted without permission, provided the credit line reads "Reprinted from UNODA Occasional Papers" and specifies the number of the Occasional Paper concerned. Notification to the following email address would be highly appreciated: unoda-web@un.org.

Symbols of United Nations documents are composed of capital letters combined with figures. These documents are available in the official languages of the United Nations at http://ods.un.org. Specific disarmament-related documents can also be accessed through the disarmament reference collection at https://www.un.org/disarmament/publications/library/.

Editor's note on photographs used in this publication. The photographs displayed in this publication of the three special sessions of the General Assembly on disarmament in 1978, 1982 and 1988 represent all that were available in the United Nations Photo Library. No photographs were omitted and no editorial decisions were made regarding exclusion or inclusion. The only decision made by the editors was page placement. Photo credits: UN Photo (John Isaac, Miguel Jimenez, Saw Lwin and Yutaka Nagata).

Author

Randy J. Rydell, PhD, Executive Advisor of Mayors for Peace, served as Senior Political Affairs Officer in UNODA (previously Department for Disarmament Affairs) from 1998 to 2014. This text is an expanded and updated version of a statement made by the author on 29 March 2016 to the Open-ended Working Group on the fourth special session of the General Assembly devoted to disarmament.

This publication is available from
www.un.org/disarmament

UNITED NATIONS PUBLICATION
Sales No. E.16.IX.9

ISBN 978-92-1-142315-0
eISBN 978-92-1-058458-6

Contents

Contents

Foreword

The General Assembly held three special sessions devoted to disarmament, in 1978, 1982 and 1988, and has been calling for a fourth since 1995.

Three Open-ended Working Groups (OEWG) to consider the objectives and an agenda for a fourth special session have been convened; the most recent one commenced its work in March 2016 and will conclude in July 2017.

At the beginning of the March 2016 meeting, Mr. Fernando Luque Márquez of Ecuador, Chair of the OEWG, asked Dr. Randy J. Rydell to present a historical overview of the three special sessions and to provide an assessment of the process. That presentation, followed by a lively two-hour question and answer period in a conference room full of delegates, is the basis for this publication.

Dr. Rydell's research and scholarship on this topic are indisputable. In the pages that follow, he not only describes what took place here at the United Nations in the 1970s and 1980s, as delegations debated ways to move disarmament and its machinery forward, but also adds contextual brushstrokes, highlights key speakers, examines foundational work that led to the special sessions and elaborates on the sessions' successes and shortcomings.

Anyone who knows Dr. Rydell will attest to his unswerving commitment to the mutually supportive goals of disarmament and non-proliferation. For 16 years until his retirement in September 2014, he worked as a Senior Political Affairs Officer in the Office for Disarmament Affairs at the United Nations. In that role he provided key advice to all of my predecessors. We are proud of and grateful for his wise and reliable counsel.

Dr. Rydell also held key positions in the Weapons of Mass Destruction Commission (Blix Commission) and the Arms Control Association in Washington, D.C. He worked for

United States Senator John Glenn from 1987 to 1998, staffing the Committee on Governmental Affairs of the United States Senate, where he contributed to the drafting and subsequent enactment of the Nuclear Proliferation Prevention Act of 1994. He was an international political analyst at the Lawrence Livermore National Laboratory from 1980 to 1986, studying the challenges of the global spread of nuclear weapons. He received his PhD in Political Science from Princeton (1980).

I am very grateful for his contribution to the UNODA Occasional Paper series.

Kim Won-soo
Under-Secretary-General
High Representative for Disarmament Affairs
October 2016

Introduction

At the third special session of the General Assembly devoted to disarmament held at United Nations Headquarters on 31 May 1988, J.M. Lekhanya (Lesotho) addresses the Assembly. Seated behind him, from left, are Secretary-General Javier Perez de Cuellar, General Assembly President Peter Florin (German Democratic Republic) and Joseph Verner Reed, Under-Secretary-General for Political and General Assembly Affairs and Secretariat Services.

Introduction

As of 2016, the General Assembly has met in 29 special sessions, with the tenth, twelfth and fifteenth devoted exclusively to disarmament. This paper provides some historical background on these particular special sessions (known by their familiar acronyms, SSOD I, SSOD II and SSOD III) and also discusses efforts to convene an SSOD IV. Emerging from this history is how the General Assembly—the closest entity to a universal democratic political arena in the United Nations system—has used these special sessions to enable all Member States to participate in the process of developing or strengthening global norms in disarmament. While these special sessions complement work done elsewhere in the multilateral disarmament machinery, their "value added" is in the comprehensive scope of their deliberations— they enable consideration of how the various parts of the disarmament puzzle fit together in a coherent whole.

Mandates

The General Assembly's mandate to meet in special sessions is briefly defined in Article 20 of the Charter, which provides that the General Assembly shall meet in such sessions "as occasion may require" and that the Secretary-General shall convoke such sessions at the request of the Security Council or a majority of Members of the United Nations.

In practice, the General Assembly has interpreted its mandate to meet in special sessions devoted to disarmament in conjunction with its other relevant mandates in the Charter, in particular its broad authority under Article 10 to "discuss" any questions or matters either within the scope of the Charter or relating to the powers and functions of any United Nations organs, and to "make recommendations" on such issues to Member States or to the Security Council. It has specific authority under Article 11 (1) to "consider the general principles of co-operation ... governing disarmament and the regulation of armaments, and may make recommendations with regard to such principles to the Members or to the Security Council or to both". It may discuss and make recommendations on any other questions relating to the maintenance of international peace and security, unless the Security Council is addressing a specific dispute or situation (Article 11 (2)). In addition, the General Assembly may call the attention of the Security Council to situations that are likely to endanger international peace and security (Article 11 (3)). It may also initiate studies and make recommendations for the purpose of promoting international cooperation in the political field and encouraging the progressive development of international law (Article 13).

The mandate to convene a special session specifically on disarmament is contained in a resolution adopted by the General Assembly, which typically contains a decision to convene such a session and identifies issues for its consideration. It may also contain a date and venue for the event or establish a Preparatory Committee for that special session. By tradition, the President of the special session is the President of the General Assembly.

In terms of rules of procedure, the rules of the General Assembly apply to the special sessions, although in practice a custom has evolved under which the special session shall, "as far as possible", make substantive decisions or recommendations by consensus.

Early history

The idea of convening a special session of the General Assembly on disarmament was originally contained in the Belgrade Declaration issued in 1961 at the First Conference of Heads of State or Government of Non-Aligned Countries; it called for either a special session or a world disarmament conference. Meeting in Cairo in 1964, the Second Conference of non-aligned countries issued a similar call. At the Conference of Ministers for Foreign Affairs of Non-Aligned Countries, held in Lima in August 1975, the proposal was reformulated into a recommendation that, if a world disarmament conference proved not to be possible, a special session of the General Assembly should be convened. A version of this position was echoed at the Fifth Conference of Heads of State or Government of Non-Aligned Countries, held in Colombo in 1976. It provided that *pending* the convening of a world disarmament conference, the non-aligned countries should support a special session of the General Assembly on disarmament. The decision to convene such a session (and to establish its Preparatory Committee) appeared in resolution 31/189 B, which the General Assembly adopted on 21 December 1976 without a vote.[1]

The conceptual roots of the SSODs, however, extend back to 1946, when the Security Council and General Assembly first recognized the twin goals of eliminating weapons of mass destruction (nuclear, chemical and biological) and the limitation and regulation of conventional arms and military expenditures. The original United Nations Disarmament Commission was established in 1952 in an early attempt to pursue a single "comprehensive" treaty accomplishing both of these aims. Ironically, efforts in

---

[1] This discussion relies on an account published in the *United Nations Disarmament Yearbook* (1976), p. 35 ff.

the United Nations to advance "general and complete disarmament under effective international control" (or GCD, which has been on the General Assembly's agenda since 1959) culminated in 1961, the same year as the Belgrade Declaration. Afterwards, GCD gave way to a series of so-called "partial measures". Nevertheless, the Final Document of SSOD I (see annex II) designated GCD as the "ultimate goal" of the disarmament process and the term can be found in a dozen multilateral and regional treaties. It is noteworthy that the substantive issues addressed in all of the SSODs mirror the full agenda of GCD, including the establishment of a link between disarmament and the wider security system based on the Charter, featuring at its core the primary norms against the threat or use of force and requiring the peaceful resolution of disputes.

The special sessions
of the General Assembly
devoted to disarmament

The special sessions of the General Assembly devoted to disarmament

Overview

Based on statements in the General Assembly, the writings of disarmament experts and views of non-governmental organizations (NGOs), the prevailing judgment of the international community is that SSOD I was a "success". This conclusion is based both on the scope of the substantive and organizational issues it addressed and the fact that the session was able to produce a consensus Final Document (see annex II).

This appraisal, however, assumes that the "outcome" of that special session was merely the successful production of a Final Document. There is far less agreement that SSOD I was a "success" based on the track record of implementation of its decisions and recommendations by Member States. This is especially apparent in the number of statements made at SSOD II reflecting quite negatively on the glaring discrepancy between the visionary goals agreed in SSOD I and the lack of progress in achieving them.

The verdict on SSOD II is generally that it was deeply disappointing, largely because of its failure to produce a consensus Final Document (only a "Concluding Document") and because of its very modest substantive achievements. Many speakers attributed the lack of consensus to the unfavourable state of international relations at the time, including tensions between the United States and the Soviet Union, especially after the latter's invasion of Afghanistan in late 1979, growing signs in the early 1980s of the aggravation of the nuclear arms race between the superpowers, tensions over the deployment of intermediate range missiles in Europe and growing disagreements on strategic missile defence.

Most commentators on SSOD III also view it as a disappointment, as it was not even able to reach a consensus on a concluding document. Some observers, however, have tempered this judgment by noting such factors as the number of speakers addressing the subtleties of the relationship between disarmament and international security, the statements calling for a wider non-weapons-based approach to security, the large number of proposals by national delegations, and, at all three special sessions, the robust and enthusiastic participation by civil society.

SSOD I (23 May to 30 June 1978)

Substantively, the basic primacy of SSOD I in the hierarchy of these special sessions relates to the ability of its participants to reach a consensus on fundamental principles and priorities for disarmament and in constructing the organizational architecture needed for subsequent work in the United Nations disarmament community. It essentially defined a detailed "division of labour" in that machinery, saying who should do what, and while institutional changes in this machinery have certainly occurred since 1978, the basic outline remains largely intact in 2016, as indeed the consensus on fundamental priorities also continues to earn widespread if not universal support.

The Final Document from SSOD I has also been widely praised for the quality of its draftsmanship. Phillip Noel-Baker, who received the Noble Peace Prize in 1959 for his work on disarmament, called it "the greatest state paper of all time".[2] Part of its greatness stemmed from its sheer size, inclusivity and high-level participation. In his opening statement to SSOD I on 23 May 1978, Secretary-General Kurt Waldheim called the event "the largest, most representative meeting ever convened to consider the problem of disarmament" and his closing statement on 30 June was no less laudatory, calling the special session "the most extensive and useful discussion of disarmament on a world-wide basis that has yet been held". In his own closing statement the same day, the conference President, Lazar Mojsov, called the event "the most representative gathering ever in the history of international relations directed exclusively to questions of halting the arms race

---

[2] Quoted by Alfonso García Robles, "Foreword" to Homer Jack, *Disarm or Die: The Second UN Special Session on Disarmament* (New York: World Conference on Religion and Peace, 1983), p. 11. [Jack, 1983].

and opening new avenues for more active and effective negotiations in disarmament", adding that the debate "was held at the highest level ever of the international dialogue on disarmament".[3]

Even the United States General Accounting Office's report on the SSOD concluded, "the United Nations special session on disarmament focused the attention of virtually every country on arms control and disarmament for the first time since the 1932 General Disarmament Conference of the League of Nations".[4]

This success was due to many factors, including the skilful leadership of Carlos Ortiz de Rozas (Argentina), who chaired the Preparatory Committee. After five sessions of the Committee, its 54 Member States had produced an outline of what would be the structure of the Final Document (Introduction, Declaration, Programme of Action and Machinery) along with agreement on many substantive provisions—although the Chair noted that the draft contained a "forest of brackets".[5]

Some statistics offer additional clues of the overall importance of SSOD I. All 149 United Nations Member States at the time were in attendance. In the general debate, 123 States participated, including 20 Heads of State or Government, 51 foreign ministers and many other high-ranking officials.

---

[3] The Waldheim and Mojsov statements are found in *Disarmament Review*, vol. I, no. 2, October 1978, pp. 3-13.

[4] General Accounting Office, "United Nations Special Session on Disarmament: A Forum for International Participation", Report ID-79-27, 3 July 1979, p. i.

[5] Carlos Ortiz de Rozas, cited in Richard Hudson, "'Most useful ever' or 'elephant death dance'", *Bulletin of the Atomic Scientists*, September 1978, p. 57.

Conference President Mojsov spoke for many when he said in his opening statement on 23 May 1978 that he "was convinced that the United Nations has the capacity to influence the creation of a new climate and set a new course in the quest for solutions to disarmament problems".[6] This sentiment was reflected in the Final Document, which stated, "the United Nations has a central role and primary responsibility in the sphere of disarmament".[7]

Some specific results included the following:

- Re-establishment of the United Nations Disarmament Commission and its conversion into a purely deliberative organ of the General Assembly.

- Establishment of the Committee (later "Conference") on Disarmament in Geneva as the world's "single multilateral disarmament negotiating forum".

- A mandate for the Committee on Disarmament to elaborate a "comprehensive programme of disarmament", a subject also given to the Disarmament Commission.

- An agreement to limit the agenda of the General Assembly's First Committee exclusively to disarmament and related issues of international security.

- Approval of the establishment of the United Nations Institute for Disarmament Research (established in 1980).

- A request to the Secretary-General to establish an advisory board of eminent persons for disarmament studies (which later became the Advisory Board

---

[6] Ibid, p. 8.
[7] See annex II, para. 27.

on Disarmament Matters), following a proposal in Secretary-General Waldheim's opening statement.

- Establishment of the United Nations Programme of Fellowships on Disarmament.

- Establishment of Disarmament Week.

- Support for strengthening the role of the Secretariat's Centre for Disarmament, especially with respect to the provision of public information and disarmament education.

- The establishment of GCD as the "ultimate objective" of the disarmament process, and the designation of nuclear disarmament as having the "highest priority".

Reflecting on his experience as Chair of the Preparatory Committee, Ambassador Ortiz de Rozas credited delegations for their flexibility and willingness to compromise. He underscored in particular the importance of dialogue, saying "So long as there is the will to maintain a dialogue and the dialogue is, in fact, maintained, divergences of view can be the starting-point for renewed attempts to make progress in the common endeavour to achieve disarmament."[8] The *United Nations Disarmament Yearbook* came to a similar conclusion about the Preparatory Committee, describing its work as having been "held in a business-like atmosphere and in a spirit of constructive cooperation which enabled it to adopt all its recommendations by consensus".[9] A year later, it concluded that the SSOD was successful because it contributed to a "better understanding of the issues involved", which helped to generate an "atmosphere" of

---

[8] Carlos Ortiz de Rozas, "The Special Session", *Disarmament Review*, vol. I, no. 1, May 1978, p. 9.
[9] *United Nations Disarmament Yearbook* (1977), p. 26.

"cooperation and mutual accommodation", in a "spirit of seeking mutually acceptable solutions" and, as a result, "concessions were made by all parties".[10]

According to that yearbook, one of the most important decisions made at the special session was to include the list of national disarmament proposals as an integral part of the text of the Final Document (para. 125). This provision requested the Secretary-General to forward these proposals with the rest of the report to the appropriate multilateral deliberative and negotiating organs. The yearbook concluded that this provision "facilitated the adoption of the Final Document by consensus".[11]

One of the most significant substantive results of SSOD I was to revive a fully "comprehensive approach" to disarmament—an approach that had been largely abandoned since GCD was eclipsed by the "partial measures" approach in the early 1960s. The true test of this approach, however, would require the development of a "comprehensive programme for disarmament", a test that Member States were unable to pass by the time of SSOD II.

---

[10] *United Nations Disarmament Yearbook* (1978), p. 74.
[11] Ibid., p. 76.

Joseph N. Garba
Commissioner for External Affairs of Nigeria
28 May 1978

Malcolm Fraser
Prime Minister of Australia
5 June 1978

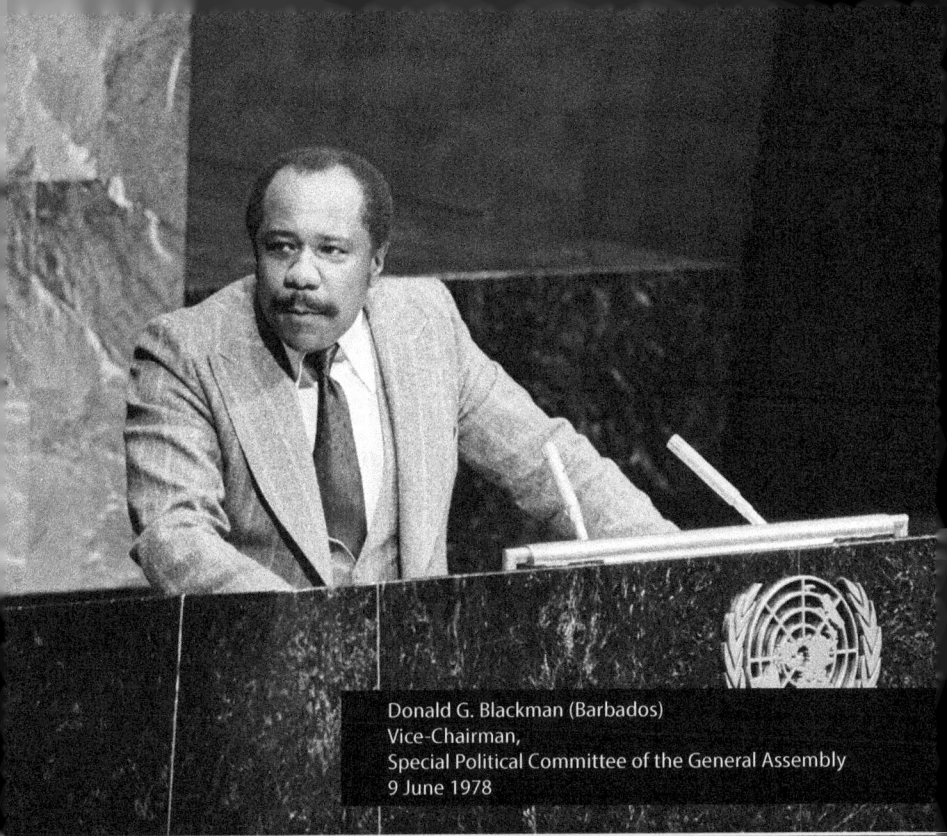

Donald G. Blackman (Barbados)
Vice-Chairman,
Special Political Committee of the General Assembly
9 June 1978

Pierre Elliott Trudeau
Prime Minister of Canada
26 May 1978

Valery Giscard d'Estaing
President of the Republic of France
25 May 1978

Hugo Scheltema, Permanent Representative of the Netherlands to the United Nations, and William B. Buffum, Under-Secretary-General for Political and General Assembly Affairs
25 May 1978

Sypros Kyprianou
President of the Republic of Cyprus
24 May 1978

Mohammed Saleh Motee'a
Minister for Foreign Affairs of Democratic Yemen
5 June 1978

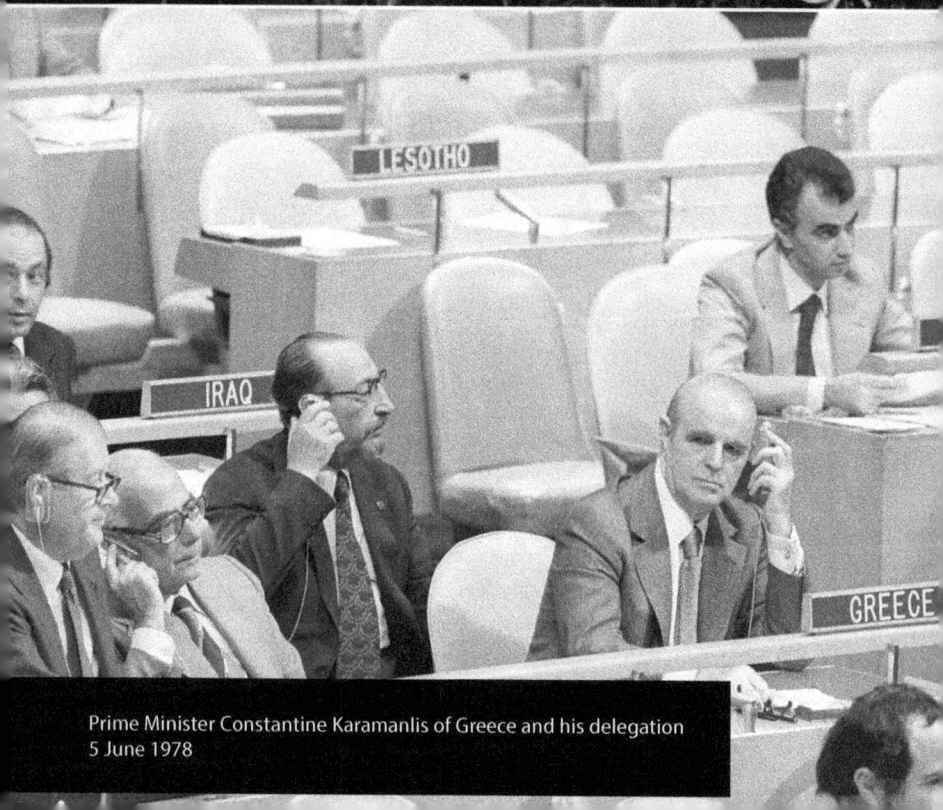

Prime Minister Constantine Karamanlis of Greece and his delegation
5 June 1978

SSOD II (7 June to 10 July 1982)

Most observers, from both the diplomatic and civil society communities, view SSOD II as at best a disappointment and at worst a failure of some historic dimensions. Ironically, this judgment seems to have formed a true consensus, where it was lacking elsewhere in this field.

The highly respected Nobel Peace Laureate, Alfonso García Robles, wrote that the SSOD I Final Document had "remained a dead letter" in implementation.[12] He said the General Assembly's advice at SSOD I "has been totally ignored" and that SSOD II had "failed hopelessly" to achieve its aim of a comprehensive programme for disarmament. In sum, he found the special session to have been an "unfortunate experience".[13]

Conference President Ismat Kittani (Iraq), in his opening statement to SSOD II, asked what had been done in disarmament since 1978 and he answered, "Nothing ... not a single weapon has been destroyed ... Nothing of significance has been done ... It is a sorry record of failure."[14]

William Epstein, a senior former member of the United Nations disarmament secretariat, concluded that "There is really no political will amongst the major powers to achieve disarmament."[15]

The NGO views were no less sparing. Homer Jack, then the long-time Chair of the NGO Committee on Disarmament at the United Nations, wrote "Never in the history of disarmament deliberations have so many worked so hard

---

[12] Jack, 1983, p. 11.
[13] Ibid., p. 12.
[14] Ibid., p. 34.
[15] Ibid., p. 215.

to produce so little."[16] He called it an "abject failure"[17] and an "unmitigated failure".[18] Jozef Goldblat, senior researcher with the Stockholm International Peace Research Institute, called SSOD II "a sad non-event".[19] Richard Hudson, editor of *Disarmament Times*, concluded "we really got a mammoth failure this time".[20] Alan Geyer, executive director of the Churches' Center for Theology and Public Policy, called the event "a deeply distressing political fiasco".[21]

Even the conclusion of the Concluding Document noted dryly that "developments since 1978 have not lived up to the hopes engendered by the tenth special session" and the results of SSOD I "have not been generally observed".[22]

The two most notable failures of this special session were its inability to fulfil its key SSOD I mandates of developing a comprehensive programme of disarmament and of not reaching a consensus on the implementation of the SSOD I decisions and recommendations since 1978. Its main substantive achievements included the launch of the World Disarmament Campaign, which enhanced the role of the United Nations in providing public information on disarmament, in promoting disarmament education and in fostering closer relations between the United Nations disarmament secretariat and civil society; another achievement was reaching a consensus to reaffirm the purposes and principles of SSOD I.[23]

---

[16] Ibid., p. 13.
[17] Ibid., p. 13.
[18] Ibid., p. 216.
[19] Ibid., p. 216.
[20] Ibid., p. 216.
[21] Ibid., p. 216.
[22] SSOD II Concluding Document, A/S-12/32, para. 59.
[23] The SSOD II "Concluding Document" is in document A/S-12/32 of 9 July 1982.

Yet despite the unimpressive track record in disarmament since 1978, SSOD II was still a major event insofar as it brought together both high-level government officials and thousands of civil society representatives to consider how to advance disarmament goals. At the general debate, 139 speakers took part, including 18 Heads of State or Government, one deputy Head of State, 44 foreign ministers and other heads of delegations.[24] In addition, over 3,000 NGO representatives registered at the session and 77 delivered oral statements to the session's Ad Hoc Committee.[25] The meetings took place at a time of great public support for disarmament, including a historic march in New York on 12 June 1982 consisting of a million participants. The contrast between this groundswell of support from civil society and the meagre achievements of SSOD II led Homer Jack to remark on the "seeming irrelevance of public opinion on [SSOD II]".[26] He added that "the fact is that NGOs have made little impact on the disarmament policies of States as reflected in the UN, either at the two special sessions or in other UN bodies ... NGOs in the UN system have recognized that their pressure counts more in national capitals than in the UN itself".[27]

Although the session adjourned with a wide variety of substantive issues left unresolved, speakers did show some signs of coalescing at least on certain specific goals, such as the importance of verification, the need for treaties to ban nuclear tests and chemical weapons, the importance of non-proliferation efforts and the need for progress in conventional arms control. Furthermore, some support was expressed for broader, non-military approaches to security

---

[24] *United Nations Disarmament Yearbook* (1982), p. 15.
[25] Jack, 1983, pp. 169, 183.
[26] Ibid., p. 13.
[27] Ibid., p. 181.

(the Palme Commission had recently completed its report[28] stressing the theme of "common security") and for the work of the Secretary-General and Centre for Disarmament Affairs. The Soviet Union announced at this meeting that it was adopting a "no first use" nuclear doctrine. The nuclear "freeze" proposal, then being actively promoted by civil society, was supported in many statements. And many delegations praised the Disarmament Fellows programme as one of the brighter legacies of SSOD I. Finally, the Concluding Document endorsed the goal of convening an SSOD III at a date to be decided by the General Assembly, which turned out to be 1988.

---

[28] The Independent Commission on Disarmament and Security Issues (Palme Commission), *Common Security: A Blueprint for Survival* (NY: Simon and Schuster, 1982).

Margaret Thatcher
Prime Minister of the United Kingdom
23 June 1982

Salem Saleh Mohammed
Minister for Foreign Affairs of Democratic Yemen
8 June 1982

Mohamed Abdulaziz Sallam
Permanent Representative of Yemen Arab Republic
21 June 1982

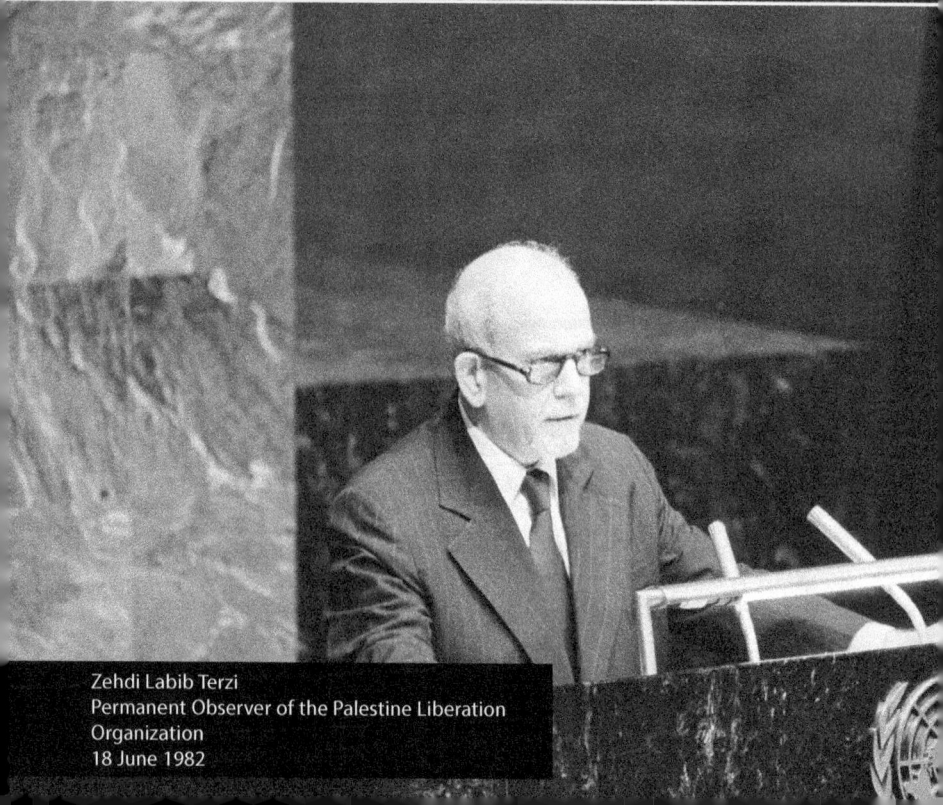

Zehdi Labib Terzi
Permanent Observer of the Palestine Liberation
Organization
18 June 1982

Philip Noel-Baker
International Association for the Work of Dr. Albert Schweitzer
24 June 1982

Ronald Reagan
President of the United States
17 June 1982

SSOD III (31 May to 26 June 1988)

The international diplomatic "climate" for considering disarmament issues was far more favourable in 1988 than in 1982. The United States and Soviet Union had just concluded a year earlier the Intermediate Nuclear Force (INF) Treaty, which broke new ground both in achieving the elimination of an entire class of nuclear-weapon delivery systems and in establishing a joint intrusive system to verify compliance. In 1986, Presidents Ronald Reagan and Mikhail Gorbachev met and discussed nuclear disarmament in Reykjavik. Talks were under way on conventional arms reduction in Europe. Progress was being reported on a START treaty. In 1986, the Rarotonga Treaty entered into force, creating a nuclear-weapon-free zone in the South Pacific. And serious efforts were ongoing to conclude treaties outlawing nuclear tests and chemical weapons, as endorsed at SSOD II.

The Concluding Document, without a substantive consensus, was adopted as General Assembly document A/S-15/50 on 25 June 1988. It contained a summary of the session's administrative details along with a list of proposals submitted by Member States and another list of NGOs and research institutes that participated in the special session.

Reactions to the inability of SSOD III to reach a consensus final document attracted several contrasting commentaries, more so than the virtually universally negative reception to SSOD II.

Representing the views of the Quaker Geneva Office, Peter Herby published a commentary entitled "UN disarmament session fizzles", which reported that the session was "without any obvious results" and that it reflected "deep basic differences".[29] The issues covered by these differences included language relating to the nuclear programmes of Israel and South Africa, the relationship between disarmament and development, the question of naval armaments and certain regional issues (namely, contrasting language over the extent that regional nuclear-weapon-free zones contribute to international security).

Herby, however, did recognize several more positive developments at this session, including widespread agreement on language relating to a United Nations verification study, support for the United Nations Department for Disarmament Affairs, the nuclear test ban, nuclear non-proliferation, conventional arms control, support for the notion of "common security" and for an enhanced role for the United Nations Secretary-General. He judged the overall debate as "notable for its mature, focused, and mostly positive" nature, which was "much less confrontational than the 1982 special session".[30] He suggested that reports from future sessions should be limited to focusing on "new areas of consensus, specific disagreements, and important new substantive proposals". He also suggested that future sessions "should arise from exceptional circumstances and unusual opportunities" and should not be scheduled "so far in advance".[31] (The General Assembly had decided in 1983 to convene an SSOD III "not later than 1988".)[32]

The President of the conference, Peter Florin (German Democratic Republic) had a more positive assessment

---

[29] Peter Herby, "UN Disarmament Session Fizzles", *Bulletin of the Atomic Scientists*, September 1988, p. 6.

[30] Ibid., p. 6.

[31] Ibid., p. 7.

[32] General Assembly resolution 38/73 I, 15 December 1983, adopted without a vote.

of the special session.[33] Florin termed SSOD III as "a major event in the world Organization's history of dealing [with disarmament]". He said the statements revealed a deeper understanding of the complex relationship between disarmament and international security, of the growing interdependence in the world, of humanitarian dimensions of disarmament (a theme that would notably reappear at the United Nations after 2010), and of growing support for "common security". He termed SSOD III as "a genuine clearing-house for the international dialogue on disarmament". And he concluded that the Final Document of SSOD I "continues to be the principal expression of the international community's determination to proceed along the road of binding and effective international agreements in the field of disarmament".

Yasushi Akashi, the United Nations Under-Secretary-General for Disarmament Affairs, concluded that SSOD III "only temporarily set back" disarmament efforts, challenging a view reported in the *New York Times* that the result was "another damaging blow" to United Nations efforts in this field.[34] He said he was "disappointed" but not "discouraged", given that Member States did share much common ground at the event; he saw the emergence of a "common outlook" on disarmament, despite the lack of a consensus. He was impressed by the high-level attendance at the event, including the fact that some 200 NGO representatives had applied to speak. He viewed the session as a "chapter" in "humanity's search for a more secure world, free from weapons of mass destruction and the threat of annihilation". Elsewhere, he told

---

[33] Peter Florin, *Disarmament Review*, vol. XI, no. 3, Autumn 1988, pp. 8-16. [Florin]

[34] Yasushi Akashi, "Is There Still Life After SSOD III?", *Disarmament Review*, vol. XI, no. 3, Autumn 1988, p. 18.

reporters, "the United Nations did not fail ... the membership failed the United Nations".[35]

The agreed agenda of this session was similar to its predecessors: a general debate; a review and appraisal of the current international situation; an assessment of implementation of the decisions and recommendations of the previous two special sessions; consideration of the comprehensive programme of disarmament; trends in the disarmament process; the role of the United Nations; the relationship between disarmament and development; and the opportunity to adopt a final document.[36]

The general debate took place over 20 meetings with 135 speakers, including 23 Heads of State or Government, one Vice-President, 6 deputy prime ministers and 61 foreign ministers. The Committee of the Whole heard statements from 87 NGOs and 20 research institutes.

The evolving structure and content of the draft final document revealed considerable areas of agreement among the Member States. The *United Nations Disarmament Yearbook* reported that the introduction was "by and large agreed", that the assessment section was "largely cleared" (except for references to the universal application of the principles of the SSOD I Final Document) and that the machinery section was the "least problem".[37] The most difficult section was on "Directions for the Future"—again, with some disagreements over references to SSOD I, disputes over language on Israel and South Africa, the contributions of regional nuclear-weapon-free zones and

---

[35] Yasushi Akashi, in Associated Press, "Says Nuclear Worries Caused Discord at Disarmament Session," 27 June 1988.
[36] This summary of the agenda and participation relies upon the *United Nations Disarmament Yearbook* (1988), p. 39.
[37] Ibid., p. 77.

zones of peace to disarmament, the role of the Secretary-General in investigating the use of chemical weapons and the relationship between disarmament and development.

After SSOD III adjourned without a consensus, the General Assembly adopted a resolution on the special session that, while acknowledging that the "general situation with regard to armament is far from satisfactory", went on to identify several positive developments at the session, including that it considered that the session "served the purpose of increasing awareness of the areas where future efforts should be concentrated and underscored the urgency that States should work resolutely for the common cause of curbing the arms race, particularly in the nuclear field, and achieving disarmament". It added that the deliberations "can provide a new direction and impetus for these efforts".[38]

---

[38] General Assembly resolution 43/77 B of 7 December 1988, by a vote of 152 in favour to none against, with two abstentions (United States and United Kingdom).

Abdul Aziz Al-Dali
Minister of Foreign Affairs of Democratic Yemen
3 June 1988

Ahmed Mohamed El-Eryani
Deputy Minister of Foreign Affairs of the Yemen Arab Republic
7 June 1988

Joe Clark
Secretary of State for External Affairs of Canada
13 June 1988

Rajiv Gandhi
Prime Minister of India
9 June 1988

Edwin Johan Sedoc
Foreign Minister of Suriname
6 June 1988

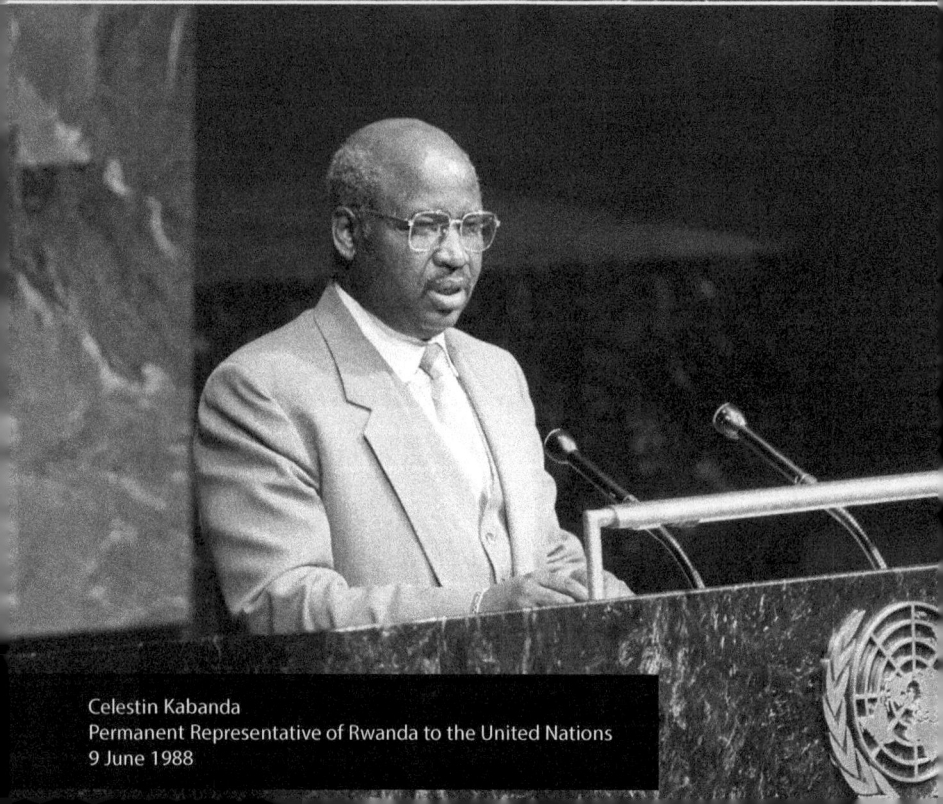
Celestin Kabanda
Permanent Representative of Rwanda to the United Nations
9 June 1988

Harri Holkeri, Prime Minister of Finland. Seated behind him, from left, are Secretary-General Javier Perez de Cuellar, General Assembly President Peter Florin (German Democratic Republic) and Joseph Verner Reed, Under-Secretary-General for Political and General Assembly Affairs and Secretariat Services. 2 June 1988

Humayun Rasheed Choudhury
Minister for Foreign Affairs of Bangladesh
14 June 1988

Lasting legacy of the three special sessions

In his remarks after the conclusion of SSOD III, conference President Peter Florin stated, "The decisive question for assessing the third Special Session should be: Did it advance the process of disarmament; did it give it a fresh impetus?"[39] The same question could be asked about each of the other special sessions and, of these, the one that is widely viewed as the most successful was followed by many years of disappointments, disillusionment, frustration and a pervasive climate of mistrust, suspected bad faith and what have been virtually universally seen as "meagre results" beyond the adoption of the Final Document itself. Florin's central question calls for assessments of special sessions to focus less on whether the session was able to produce a consensus final document than on what concrete accomplishments were later achieved by fulfilling decisions or recommendations reached in the previous special sessions.

In other words, a final document is best seen not as an end itself, but as a blueprint or reference point for assessing the subsequent behaviour of Member States in living up to their commitments. In this sense, a final document of a special session offers not just a set of goals to pursue, but some yardsticks for gauging whether the policies, priorities and practices of States are consistent with those goals. Special sessions are largely about establishing accountability for past commitments, clarifying or reaffirming principles and goals, and developing new multilateral disarmament norms.

They are also part of a larger process of building the legitimacy of disarmament as a worthy national, regional and multilateral goal to pursue, as part of the Charter's larger system for maintaining international peace and security.

---

[39] Florin, p.10.

Disarmament's procedural legitimacy arises from the ability of special sessions (and deliberations elsewhere in the United Nations disarmament machinery) to afford opportunities for all States—especially small- and medium-sized States—to participate in the global process of disarmament. This helps to explain the strong support that these special sessions have had, from the start, from the non-aligned countries.

Similarly, the ability of representatives of civil society to participate—to have a voice and to circulate their publications—also helps to strengthen the legitimacy of disarmament by ensuring that States and groups have a fair opportunity to participate in the process of developing, maintaining and strengthening global disarmament norms. And the greater this participation, the greater will be the likelihood that the specific norms that are adopted will also be fair in substance, rather than embodying double standards or conferring special benefits for some or special costs for others. The lack of significant impact of NGO advocacy in 1982 on the outcome of SSOD II offers no basis at all for predictions about the future, especially if those efforts expand to include international networks that cut across many sectors of society, well beyond the peace groups, including parliamentarians, mayors, doctors, lawyers, women's groups, environmentalists, religious leaders, former military personnel and government officials and, one day, maybe even the business community.

One of the most important contributions of the special sessions is their role in providing a high-profile forum for the "collective legitimization" of disarmament, especially nuclear disarmament, as a "global public good of the highest order", in the words of Secretary-General Ban Ki-moon.[40]

---

[40] Ban Ki-moon, address to EastWest Institute, United Nations, 24 October 2008.

Such sessions also offer an opportunity to revive the "comprehensive approach" to disarmament, which (as noted earlier) was largely abandoned by the world community in the early 1960s in favour of partial measures. SSODs have the potential to put some flesh on the bones of "general and complete disarmament under effective international control" by identifying what needs to be done, how certain parts of the disarmament enterprise are inseparable from certain other parts of that enterprise and how weapons of mass destruction disarmament and conventional arms control are synergistic and hence must be pursued simultaneously rather than sequentially in some contrived "step by step process" without an end, a plan or any credibility.

Former Secretary-General Kurt Waldheim once called for a "strategy of disarmament"—a plan of action with a clear end and specific practical measures for its achievement.[41] A special session is a superb forum for producing such a strategy that is comprehensive in substance and universal in participation to address all relevant facets of this challenge. In an article assessing SSOD I, William Epstein referred to what he called "the international security, disarmament and development triad".[42] The close relationship between these subjects has been part of the United Nations' comprehensive approach to disarmament, with roots traceable back to 1946. It helps to form what Alfonso García Robles once called "the United Nations philosophy on disarmament".[43]

These statements testify to the conceptual coherence and fundamental unity of all the various approaches to disarmament—a coherence and unity that is often missing

---

[41] Secretary-General Kurt Waldheim, opening address to SSOD I, 23 May 1978.
[42] William Epstein, "The United Nations and International Security", *Bulletin of the Atomic Scientists*, June/July 1982, p. 39.
[43] Alfonso García Robles, "Foreword" to Jack, 1983, p. 11.

from other forums in the United Nations disarmament machinery, where a piecemeal, issue-by-issue approach has become the custom, and a common understanding of these complex interrelationships is often lost. By their comprehensive focus, their high-level and universal participation, their unique role in conferring collective legitimacy to multilateral disarmament initiatives, special sessions all have important roles to play that transcend the routine deliberations elsewhere in that machinery.

Aside from their role in norm-building, these sessions serve to educate both Member States and civil society about the real issues involved—economic, technological, political, psychological and conceptual—in advancing a bona fide disarmament agenda. Their high-level participation offers opportunities for attracting media attention and focusing the attention of government bureaucracies. Their very existence can inspire the creation of outside initiatives, such as the establishment of the NGO Mayors for Peace as a result of a proposal made by Hiroshima Mayor Takeshi Araki at SSOD II—an NGO that today has members from over 7,100 cities worldwide.[44]

Special sessions also have the opportunity to put disappointments and setbacks into their proper light. Collectively, the crushing economic burdens of armaments, international sabre-rattling, weapon modernization programmes and failures to implement disarmament commitments may, in their own ways, open up new doors for progress in disarmament to occur, especially if these developments are perceived by the public and their significance for national and international peace, security and prosperity are recognized. As Secretary-General Dag

---

[44] For further details on this NGO, visit http://www.mayorsforpeace.org/english/index.html.

Hammarskjöld once observed, an armaments race—through the many burdens it imposes—"can dig its own grave".[45] It is up to Member States and civil society to make the best of such developments, in arenas such as the special sessions, to advance disarmament and to overcome common misperceptions such as that it is a utopian lost cause. Turning disappointments into fresh opportunities for progress: this is the essence of political will—that often-cited missing quantity in countless disarmament arenas.

The growing public awareness of the humanitarian consequences of the use of nuclear weapons—but also of arms races and the growing burdens of military expenditure—offers a solid foundation for reviving a comprehensive approach to disarmament. If and when this happens, there will be positive contributions to expect from special sessions of the General Assembly.

It has now been almost three decades since the last General Assembly special session on disarmament. Is the current situation a reflection of the failure of SSOD III and its predecessors? Or is it more as Yasushi Akashi suggested—a failure of Member States to live up to the multilateral norms forged in United Nations disarmament arenas? Arguably, there is nothing wrong with special sessions that the Member States do not have the power to solve. As the President of SSOD I (Lazar Mojsov) put it in his closing statement, "What we have not accomplished now, we will do later".

---

[45] Secretary-General Dag Hammarskjöld, Press Conference, New York, 6 February 1958.

Postscript

Developments relating to the special sessions devoted to disarmament since 1988

Postscript

Developments relating to the special sessions on disarmament since 1988

The disappointing outcome of SSOD III did not in any way weaken the resolve of many Member States to ensure the regular review of the decisions and recommendations of the previous SSODs and, a few years later, to consider the convening of an SSOD IV. This determination was registered in many institutions of the United Nations disarmament machinery—most notably, the General Assembly, four General Assembly Open-ended Working Groups and the United Nations Disarmament Commission.

General Assembly[46]

In terms of the General Assembly's official agenda, resolution 42/40 of 30 November 1987 placed SSOD III on its 1988 agenda, adding to existing agenda items pertaining to the follow-ups on SSOD I and II. After the failure of SSOD III, however, the General Assembly created a new agenda item covering the "Special sessions on disarmament" collectively (resolution 43/77 B of 7 December 1988).

In the years from 1989 to 1995, the General Assembly adopted numerous resolutions pertaining to the

---

[46] This section draws upon a list of previous General Assembly resolutions and decisions on an SSOD IV prepared by Katherine Prizeman of UNODA, which is attached as annex I to this present paper.

implementation of various decisions and recommendations of SSOD I and II. In 1988 alone, there were 13 separate resolutions relating to SSOD I and 8 relating to SSOD II. The subject matters varied widely, as some addressed substantive themes (e.g., disarmament and development, the nuclear freeze, nuclear disarmament and non-use of nuclear weapons) and routine annual reports of institutions established by or following the earlier SSODs, including reports dealing with the United Nations Disarmament Commission, UNIDIR and the three United Nations regional centres for peace and disarmament.

In 1994, however, the General Assembly adopted its first resolution on SSOD IV (resolution 49/75 I of 15 December 1994), in which it decided "in principle" to convene such a special session in 1997; the resolution also placed SSOD IV on the General Assembly's provisional agenda for its fiftieth session (1995). Following 1995, the primary SSOD resolutions focused specifically on SSOD IV. Three resolutions contained decisions to convene an SSOD IV in specific years.[47]

One common theme of these SSOD IV resolutions has been the inclusion of a clause recognizing that the new special session would be "subject to the emergence of a consensus on its objectives and agenda" (this language or slight variations thereof was used in the annual resolutions adopted from 1996 to 2010). While most SSOD IV resolutions have been adopted without a vote, several have been adopted with votes, typically featuring a few abstentions (e.g., 1995, 1996, 2006, 2007 and 2010); three of the eight General Assembly decisions relating to SSOD IV were voted upon, also with a few abstentions (i.e., 2012, 2014 and 2015).

---

[47] General Assembly resolutions 49/75 I (1994) and 50/70 F (1995) set the date for 1997; and resolution 51/45 C (1996) set it for 1999.

Open-ended Working Groups

Led by non-aligned Member States, efforts in the General Assembly to convene an SSOD IV have included the establishment of four Open-ended Working Groups. However, given that the Open-ended Working Groups conduct their deliberations in closed meetings, there is little official documentation of specific statements, exchanges and issues raised at these events. Nevertheless, some statements have been published and at least some documentation exists concerning the substantive issues raised.

1. 2003 Working Group: Establishment and results

The 2003 Working Group was established pursuant to General Assembly resolution 57/61, which was adopted without a vote on 22 November 2002. The Group was to consider the objectives and agenda, including the possible establishment of a preparatory committee, for an SSOD IV. Under the chairmanship of Mochamad Slamet Hidayat (Indonesia), the Group held three substantive sessions in 2003. It was however unable to reach a consensus, as stated in the Group's final report.[48] There were disagreements over the priority of disarmament relative to non-proliferation and over the interpretation of the results of SSOD I.[49]

2. 2006 Working Group: Establishment only

The 2006 Working Group was established pursuant to General Assembly resolution 59/71, which was adopted without a vote on 3 December 2004 and given a similar mandate as the 2003 Working Group. The resolution had been introduced by Malaysia on behalf of members of the

---

[48] A/57/848, 14 July 2003.
[49] *United Nations Disarmament Yearbook* (2003), p. 245.

Non-Aligned Movement. This Working Group was to hold its substantive sessions in 2006, but never officially met. The General Assembly decided on 8 December 2005 to place the issue of SSOD IV on its provisional agenda for its sixty-first session. On 6 June 2006, the General Assembly adopted decision 60/559 (introduced by Indonesia), in which it "decided to establish, at a later date, an Open-ended Working Group" to consider convening an SSOD IV.

3. 2007 Working Group: Establishment and results

The 2007 Working Group was established pursuant to resolution 61/60, which was adopted on 6 December 2006 by a vote of 175 in favour to 1 against (United States), with no abstentions. Its mandate was similar to that of the 2003 Working Group. Chaired by Alfredo Labbé (Chile), the Group met in one organizational session and three substantive sessions, for a total of 15 meetings in 2007. The Group's final report concluded that "no consensus" was reached.[50] The Chair annexed to this report his reflections on the Group's deliberations.[51] While he concluded that "the critical mass of political support necessary to convene an SSOD IV *has not yet been reached*" (emphasis in original), he also identified many areas of general agreement and suggested that the General Assembly might consider establishing a "Group of Experts" to work on the issue. On 5 December 2007, the General Assembly adopted resolution 62/29, which contained its decision to convene "the" Open-ended Working Group for its substantive sessions in 2008. When no such sessions were held in 2008, the General Assembly adopted a decision sponsored by Indonesia on 11 September of that year "to continue work on convening those sessions ... as soon as

---

[50] A/AC.268/2007/2, 31 August 2007.
[51] Ibid., annex V.

possible".[52] The General Assembly adopted decision 63/519 on 2 December 2008, in which it placed the SSOD IV issue on the agenda for its sixty-fourth session (2009), and decision 64/515 on 2 December 2009, in which it placed the issue on the agenda for its sixty-fifth session (2010).

4. 2010 Working Group: Establishment and results

The 2010 Working Group was established pursuant to resolution 65/66, which was adopted on 8 December 2010 by a vote of 178 in favour to none against, with 5 abstentions (France, Israel, Palau, United Kingdom and United States). In the resolution, the General Assembly decided that the Working Group should hold an organizational session as soon as possible to set dates for substantive sessions in 2011 and 2012. On 3 December 2012, the General Assembly adopted decision 67/518, in which it asked the Working Group to hold an organizational session to set dates for substantive sessions in 2013 and 2014. The decision was adopted by a vote of 181 in favour to none against, with 4 abstentions (France, Israel, United Kingdom and United States). This pattern was repeated in 2014 when the General Assembly adopted decision 69/518 on 2 December 2014, providing for substantive sessions for the Working Group to occur in 2015 and 2016. That vote was 175 in favour to none against, with 4 abstentions (France, Israel, United Kingdom and United States). The most recent General Assembly action was the adoption of decision 70/551 on 23 December 2015, by which the Working Group would set a date for its substantive sessions in 2016 and 2017. The vote was 149 in favour to none against, with 5 abstentions (Central African Republic, France, Israel, Netherlands and United States). The Working Group (now called the 2016 Working Group) held its first

---

[52] General Assembly decision 62/552 of 11 September 2008.

substantive session on 28 March 2016; future sessions are planned for July 2016 and June 2017.[53]

United Nations Disarmament Commission

The United Nations Disarmament Commission addressed SSOD IV during four consecutive years, from 1996 to 1999. Its initial mandate came indirectly from resolution 50/72 D of 12 December 1995, which contained the agenda for the Commission's 1996 session; the resolution left open the selection of two of the three agenda items, noting that these would be decided at the commission's organizational meeting, which agreed to include the SSOD IV item. The Commission's substantive deliberations began on 22 April 1996 with a call from its Chair, Wolfgang Hoffmann (Germany), for deliberations to explore "areas of convergence" as a means to overcome "divergent views" in the commission on this issue.[54] The Commission established Working Group II to address issues relating to SSOD IV. Chaired by Luvsanguiin Erdenechuluun (Mongolia), this group held 10 meetings in April and May 1996. Working papers were presented by the United States, the European Union, the Non-Aligned Movement, New Zealand and the Chair of the Working Group.[55] The Commission's meeting on 3 May 1996 focused on the work of Working Group II and reflected varying views among delegations on the objectives and timing of SSOD IV.[56]

---

[53] A/AC.268/2016/CRP.1/Rev.1, 1 April 2016.

[54] A/CN/10/PV.200, 22 April 1996.

[55] The references to these working papers are contained in the Report of the United Nations Disarmament Commission (1996), A/51/42, 22 May 1996.

[56] A/CN.10/PV.205, 3 May 1996.

On 10 December 1996, the General Assembly adopted resolution 51/47 B, in which it asked the Commission to include SSOD IV as an item for its substantive session. The Commission met from 21 April to 13 May 1997 under the chairmanship of Andelfo Garcia (Colombia). As in the previous year, a Working Group II was set up to address the SSOD IV issue, under the chairmanship of Sudjadnan Parnohadiningrat (Indonesia). This group held 12 meetings between 28 April and 9 May. Working papers were circulated by the Non-Aligned Movement, the United States, the European Union, New Zealand, China and the Chair of the Working Group. The latter consisted of a summary of key elements of proposals made during the meetings of the Working Group.[57]

By adopting resolution 52/40 B on 9 December 1997, the General Assembly welcomed the inclusion of SSOD IV as an item on the Commission's agenda for 1998. The Commission met for three weeks in April 1998 under the chairmanship of Sergei Martynov (Belarus). Working Group II (still chaired by Ambassador Parnohadiningrat) resumed its deliberations on SSOD IV during 15 meetings held between 9 and 24 April. Eleven working papers (from this and the earlier session) were circulated by the United States, the European Union, the Non-Aligned Movement, New Zealand, Canada, China and the Chair of the Working Group. The latter contained two lists of possible objectives and agenda items for SSOD IV.[58]

The last of the Commission's sessions on SSOD IV occurred in 1999 following the General Assembly's adoption of resolution 53/79 A of 4 December 1998, which included

---

[57] Report of the United Nations Disarmament Commission (1997), A/52/42, 4 June 1997.
[58] Report of the United Nations Disarmament Commission (1998), A/53/42, 24 April 1998.

SSOD IV once again as an item for the Commission's substantive agenda. The Commission was chaired in 1999 by Maged Abdelaziz (Egypt) and Working Group II was chaired by Arizal Effendi (Indonesia). The Working Group held six meetings from 14 to 29 April. The 11 working papers from earlier sessions were again circulated as documents for the Group. The Working Group held its last meeting on 29 April, having concluded that it "was not able to reach a consensus" on the objectives and agenda for SSOD IV.[59]

---

[59] Report of the United Nations Disarmament Commission (1999), A/54/42, 6 May 1999.

Concluding comment

Concluding comment

Given all the disappointments and setbacks associated with the past special sessions on disarmament—in particular concerning the implementation of agreed standards and recommendations—it is easy to conclude that these sessions offer little hope for advancing multilateral disarmament goals. Yet, as Dag Hammarskjöld used to say about disarmament, the notion of an SSOD has itself become a "hardy perennial" in the United Nations disarmament machinery. The priorities, policies and practices of individual Member States undoubtedly remain the most critical determinant of the success or failure of multilateral disarmament deliberations, which leaves the ultimate responsibility for the outcomes of those events squarely on the doorsteps of the Member States.

Yet, pending the establishment of a long-postponed "world disarmament conference", the SSOD has offered Member States a unique universal forum not just for deliberating controls over specific types of weapons, but to consider the intricate relationships between disarmament and closely related subjects of arms control, peace, security, development and, in all likelihood in future years, the environment. It offers, in short, a fitting arena for the pursuit of the long-agreed "ultimate goal" of the United Nations in disarmament—namely, general and complete disarmament under effective international control, a comprehensive approach that combines disarmament, arms control and the fundamental norms of the Charter into a unified, coherent whole. Member States in the General Assembly will, therefore, surely continue to pursue the establishment of an

SSOD IV and the full implementation of achievements made at the earlier special sessions.

This paper has attempted to explain why this is the case and why the special sessions continue to have the potential to contribute significantly to the multilateral disarmament process. There is no necessary incompatibility of pursuing a comprehensive approach and partial measures, but only if the latter are tied to concrete results and overseen by a system of regular accountability to ensure their full implementation. It is this regular process of reviewing actions to fulfil agreed commitments that offers one of the most effective responses to the secrecy that typically surrounds nuclear-weapon decision-making in all the possessor States. As a tool of multilateral disarmament diplomacy, the option of convening special sessions is here to stay. Democracy is indeed coming to disarmament.

Annexes

Annex I

List of previous General Assembly resolutions and decisions on the convening of a fourth special session of the General Assembly devoted to disarmament

Prepared by Katherine Prizeman, UNODA

49/75 I. Convening of the fourth special session of the General Assembly devoted to disarmament (1994)

The General Assembly:

OP* 1. Decides, *in principle*, [emphasis added] to convene, in 1997 if possible, the fourth special session of the General Assembly devoted to disarmament, the date to be determined at its fiftieth session;

50/70 F. Convening of the fourth special session of the General Assembly devoted to disarmament (1995)

The General Assembly:

OP 1. Decides to convene its fourth special session on disarmament in 1997, if possible, the exact date and agenda to be decided upon before the end of the current session of the General Assembly through consultations;

OP 2. Also decides to establish a Preparatory Committee to prepare a draft agenda for the special session, to examine all relevant questions relating to that session and to submit its

---

* OP = operative paragraph.

recommendations thereon to the General Assembly at its fifty-first session;

OP 3. Invites all Member States to communicate to the Secretary-General, no later than 1 April 1996, their views on the draft agenda and other relevant questions relating to the fourth special session on disarmament;

OP 4. Requests the Preparatory Committee to meet for a short organizational session before the end of the fifty-first session of the General Assembly in order, inter alia, to set the date for its substantive session;

OP 5. Also requests the Preparatory Committee to submit its progress report to the General Assembly at its fifty-first session;

51/45 C. Convening of the fourth special session of the General Assembly devoted to disarmament (1996)

The General Assembly:

OP 1. Decides, *subject to the emergence of a consensus on its objectives and agenda*, [emphasis added] to convene its fourth special session devoted to disarmament in 1999;

OP 3. Decides, subject to the outcome of deliberations concerning the fourth special session of the General Assembly devoted to disarmament at the 1997 substantive session of the Disarmament Commission, to convene a meeting of the Preparatory Committee for the Fourth Special Session of the General Assembly devoted to Disarmament before the end of the fifty-first session of the Assembly in order to set an exact date and to decide on organizational matters relating to the convening of the special session, and requests the Preparatory Committee to submit its progress report to the Assembly at its fifty-second session;

52/38 F. Fourth special session of the General Assembly on disarmament: report of the Preparatory Committee for the Fourth Special Session of the General Assembly Devoted to Disarmament (1997)

The General Assembly:

OP 1. Decides, *subject to the emergence of a consensus on its objectives and agenda*, [emphasis added] to convene the fourth special session of the General Assembly devoted to disarmament;

OP 2. Endorses the recommendation of the Disarmament Commission at its 1997 substantive session that the item entitled "Fourth special session of the General Assembly devoted to disarmament" should be included in the agenda of the Commission at its 1998 session;

OP 3. ... subject to the outcome of the deliberations at the 1998 substantive session of the Disarmament Commission, to set an exact date for and to decide on organizational matters relating to the convening of the special session.

53/77 AA. Convening of the Fourth Special Session of the General Assembly Devoted to Disarmament (1998)

The General Assembly:

OP 1. Decides, *subject to the emergence of a consensus on its objectives and agenda*, [emphasis added] to convene the fourth special session of the General Assembly devoted to disarmament;

OP 2. Endorses the report of the Disarmament Commission on its 1998 substantive session, and recommends that an item entitled "Fourth special session of the General Assembly devoted to disarmament" be included in the agenda of the Commission at its 1999 session, which should promote agreement on the agenda and timing of the special session;

OP 3. Decides to include in the provisional agenda of its fifty-fourth session the item entitled "Convening of the fourth special session of the General Assembly devoted to disarmament" and, subject to the outcome of the deliberations at the 1999 substantive session of the Disarmament Commission, to set an exact date for and to decide on organizational matters relating to the convening of the special session.

54/54 U. Convening of the Fourth Special Session of the General Assembly Devoted to Disarmament (1999)

The General Assembly:

OP 1. Decides, *subject to the emergence of a consensus on its objectives and agenda*, [emphasis added] to convene the fourth special session of the General Assembly devoted to disarmament;

OP 2. Requests the Secretary-General to seek the views of States Members of the United Nations on the objectives, agenda and timing of the special session and to report to the General Assembly at its fifty-fifth session;

55/33 M. Convening of the Fourth Special Session of the General Assembly Devoted to Disarmament (2000)

The General Assembly:

OP 1. Decides, *subject to the emergence of a consensus on its objectives and agenda*, [emphasis added] to convene the fourth special session of the General Assembly devoted to disarmament;

OP 2. Requests the Secretary-General to seek the views of States Members of the United Nations on the objectives, agenda and timing of the special session and to report to the General Assembly at its fifty-fifth session;

56/24 D. Convening of the Fourth Special Session of the General Assembly Devoted to Disarmament (2001)

The General Assembly:

OP 1. Decides, *subject to the emergence of a consensus on its objectives and agenda*, [emphasis added] to convene the fourth special session of the General Assembly devoted to disarmament;

OP 2. Requests the Secretary-General to seek the views of States Members of the United Nations on the objectives, agenda and timing of the special session and to report to the General Assembly at its fifty-fifth session;

57/61. Convening of the Fourth Special Session of the General Assembly Devoted to Disarmament (2002)

[Establishment of Open-ended Working group—see first report, A/57/848]

The General Assembly:

OP 1. Decides to establish an open-ended working group, *working on the basis of consensus*, [emphasis added] to consider the objectives and agenda, including the possible establishment of the preparatory committee, for the fourth special session of the General Assembly devoted to disarmament, taking note of the paper presented by the Chairman of Working Group II during the 1999 substantive session of the Disarmament Commission as well as the reports of the Secretary-General regarding the views of Member States on the objectives, agenda and timing of the fourth special session of the General Assembly devoted to disarmament;

OP 2. Requests the open-ended Working Group to hold an organizational session in order to set the date for its substantive sessions, and to submit a report on its work, including possible substantive recommendations, before the end of the fifty-seventh session of the General Assembly;

OP 3. Requests the Secretary-General, within existing resources, to provide the open-ended Working Group with the necessary assistance and services as may be required to discharge its tasks;

58/521. Convening of the Fourth Special Session of the General Assembly Devoted to Disarmament (2003) (decision)

The General Assembly:

(a)   Takes note of the report of the Open-ended Working Group to consider the objectives and agenda, including the possible establishment of the preparatory committee, for the fourth special session of the General Assembly devoted to disarmament and of requests made for Member States to continue consultations in this regard;

(b)   Decides to include in the provisional agenda of its fifty-ninth session the sub-item entitled "Convening of the fourth special session of the General Assembly devoted to disarmament".

59/71. Convening of the fourth special session of the General Assembly devoted to disarmament (2004)

[Establishment of OEWG, which did not meet]

The General Assembly:

OP 1. Decides to establish an open-ended working group, *working on the basis of consensus,* [emphasis added] to consider the objectives and agenda, including the possible establishment of the preparatory committee, for the fourth special session of the General Assembly devoted to disarmament, taking note of the paper presented by the Chairman of Working Group II during the 1999 substantive session of the Disarmament Commission and the written proposals and views submitted by Member States as contained in the working papers presented during the three substantive sessions of the Open-ended Working Group in 2003, as well as the reports of the Secretary-General regarding the views of Member States on the objectives, agenda and timing of the fourth special session of the General Assembly devoted to disarmament;

OP 2. Requests the Open-ended Working Group to hold an organizational session in order to set the dates for its substantive sessions in 2006, and to submit a report on its work, including possible substantive recommendations, before the end of the sixtieth session of the General Assembly;

OP 3. Requests the Secretary-General, within existing resources, to provide the Open-ended Working Group with the necessary assistance and services as may be required to discharge its tasks;

60/518. Convening of the fourth special session of the General Assembly devoted to disarmament (2005) (decision)

The General Assembly, recalling its decision 58/521 of 8 December 2003 and its resolution 59/71 of 3 December 2004, decides to include in the provisional agenda of its sixty-first session the item entitled "Convening of the fourth special session of the General Assembly devoted to disarmament".

60/559. Convening of the fourth special session of the General Assembly devoted to disarmament (2006) (decision)

The General Assembly, recalling its resolution 59/71 of 3 December 2004 and its decision 60/518 of 8 December 2005, decides to establish, at a later date, an Open-ended Working Group to consider the objectives and agenda, including the possible establishment of a preparatory committee, for the fourth special session of the General Assembly devoted to disarmament.

61/60. Convening of the fourth special session of the General Assembly devoted to disarmament (2006)

[Establishment of OEWG—see second report, A/AC.268/2007/2]

The General Assembly:

OP 1. Decides to establish an open-ended working group, *working on the basis of consensus*, [emphasis added] to consider the objectives and agenda, including the possible establishment of the preparatory committee, for the fourth special session of the General Assembly devoted to disarmament, taking note of the paper presented by the Chairman of Working Group II during the 1999 substantive session of the Disarmament Commission and the written proposals and views submitted by Member States as contained in the working papers presented during the three substantive sessions of the Open-ended Working Group in 2003 as well as the reports of the Secretary-General regarding the views of Member States on the objectives, agenda and timing of the fourth special session of the General Assembly devoted to disarmament;

OP 2. Requests the Open-ended Working Group to hold an organizational session in order to set the date for its substantive sessions in 2007 and to submit a report on its work, including possible substantive recommendations, before the end of the sixty-first session of the General Assembly;

OP 3. Requests the Secretary-General, within existing resources, to provide the Open-ended Working Group with the necessary assistance and services as may be required to discharge its tasks;

62/29. Convening of the fourth special session of the General Assembly devoted to disarmament (2007)

The General Assembly:

OP 1. Decides to convene the Open-ended Working Group, *working on the basis of consensus*, [emphasis added] to consider the objectives and agenda, including the possible establishment of the preparatory committee, for the fourth special session of the General Assembly devoted to disarmament;

OP 2. Also decides that the Open-ended Working Group shall hold its organizational session as soon as possible for the purpose of setting a date for its substantive sessions in 2008, and submit a report on its work, including possible substantive recommendations, before the end of the sixty-second session of the General Assembly;

OP 3. Requests the Secretary-General, within existing resources, to provide the Open-ended Working Group with the necessary assistance and services as may be required to discharge its tasks;

62/552. Convening of the fourth special session of the General Assembly devoted to disarmament (2008) (decision)

The General Assembly, recalling paragraph 2 of its resolution 62/29 of 5 December 2007, and noting that the Open-ended Working Group to consider the objectives and agenda, including the possible establishment of the preparatory committee, for the fourth special session of the General Assembly devoted to disarmament did not convene its organizational and substantive sessions during the sixty-second session of the General Assembly in 2008, decides to continue work on convening those sessions of the Working Group as soon as possible.

63/519. Convening of the fourth special session of the General Assembly devoted to disarmament (2008) (decision)

The General Assembly, recalling its decision 62/552 of 11 September 2008 and its resolution 62/29 of 5 December 2007, decides to include in the provisional agenda of its sixty-fourth session the item entitled "Convening of the fourth special session of the General Assembly devoted to disarmament".

64/515. Convening of the fourth special session of the General Assembly devoted to disarmament (2009) (decision)

The General Assembly, recalling its resolution 62/29 of 5 December 2007 and its decisions 62/552 of 11 September 2008 and 63/519 of 2 December 2008, decides to include in the provisional agenda of its sixty-fifth session the item entitled "Convening of the fourth special session of the General Assembly devoted to disarmament".

65/66. Convening of the fourth special session of the General Assembly devoted to disarmament (2010)

[Establishment of OEWG—see reports of 2016-2017 substantive sessions]

The General Assembly:

OP 1. Decides to convene an Open-ended Working Group, *working on the basis of consensus*, [emphasis added] to consider the objectives and agenda, including the possible establishment of the preparatory committee, for the fourth special session of the General Assembly devoted to disarmament;

OP 2. Also decides that the Open-ended Working Group shall hold its organizational session as soon as possible for the purpose of setting a date for its substantive sessions in 2011 and 2012, and submit a report on its work, including possible substantive recommendations, before the end of the sixty-seventh session of the General Assembly;

OP 3. Requests the Secretary-General, from within available resources, to provide the Open-ended Working Group with the necessary assistance and services as may be required to discharge its tasks;

67/518. Open-ended Working Group on the Fourth Special Session of the General Assembly Devoted to Disarmament (2012) (decision)

The General Assembly, recalling its resolution 65/66 of 8 December 2010, decides to:

(a) Hold, at a later date, an organizational session of the Open-ended Working Group on the Fourth Special Session of the General Assembly Devoted to Disarmament for the purpose of setting a date for its substantive sessions in 2013 and 2014, and submit a report on its work, including possible substantive recommendations, before the end of the sixty-ninth session of the General Assembly;

(b)   Include in the provisional agenda of its sixty-eighth session, under the item entitled "General and complete disarmament", a sub-item entitled "Convening of the fourth special session of the General Assembly devoted to disarmament".

69/518. Open-ended Working Group on the Fourth Special Session of the General Assembly Devoted to Disarmament (2014) (decision)

The General Assembly, recalling its resolution 65/66 of 8 December 2010 and its decision 67/518 of 3 December 2012, decides to:

(a)   Hold, at a later date, an organizational session of the Open-ended Working Group on the Fourth Special Session of the General Assembly Devoted to Disarmament for the purpose of setting a date for its substantive sessions in 2015 and 2016, and submit a report on its work, including possible substantive recommendations, before the end of the seventy-first session of the General Assembly;

(b)   Include in the provisional agenda of its seventieth session, under the item entitled "General and complete disarmament", a sub-item entitled "Convening of the fourth special session of the General Assembly devoted to disarmament".

70/551. Open-ended Working Group on the Fourth Special Session of the General Assembly Devoted to Disarmament (2015) (decision)

The General Assembly, recalling its resolution 65/66 of 8 December 2010 and its decision 69/518 of 2 December 2014, decides to:

(a)   Hold, at a later date, an organizational session of the Open-ended Working Group on the Fourth Special Session of the General Assembly Devoted to Disarmament for the purpose of setting a date for its substantive sessions in 2016 and 2017, and that the Working Group should submit a report on its work, including possible substantive recommendations, before the end of the seventy-second session of the General Assembly;

(b)   Include in the provisional agenda of its seventy-first session, under the item entitled "General and complete disarmament", a sub-item entitled "Convening of the fourth special session of the General Assembly devoted to disarmament".

Annex II

Final Document of the Tenth Special Session of the General Assembly

Excerpted from General Assembly resolution S-10/2 of 30 June 1978

Contents

I.   Introduction

1.   The attainment of the objective of security, which is an inseparable element of peace, has always been one of the most profound aspirations of humanity. States have for a long time sought to maintain their security through the possession of arms. Admittedly, their survival has, in certain cases, effectively depended on whether they could count on appropriate means of defence. Yet the accumulation of weapons, particularly nuclear weapons, today constitutes much more a threat than a protection for the future of mankind. The time has therefore come to put an end to this situation, to abandon the use of force in international relations and to seek security in disarmament, that is to say, through a gradual but effective process beginning with a reduction in the present level of armaments. The ending of the arms race and the achievement of real disarmament are tasks of primary importance and urgency. To meet this historic challenge is in the political and economic interests of all the nations and peoples of the world

as well as in the interests of ensuring their genuine security and peaceful future.

2.   Unless its avenues are closed, the continued arms race means a growing threat to international peace and security and even to the very survival of mankind. The nuclear and conventional arms build-up threatens to stall the efforts aimed at reaching the goals of development, to become an obstacle on the road of achieving the new international economic order and to hinder the solution of other vital problems facing mankind.

3.   The dynamic development of détente, encompassing all spheres of international relations in all regions of the world, with the participation of all countries, would create conditions conducive to the efforts of States to end the arms race, which has engulfed the world, thus reducing the danger of war. Progress on détente and progress on disarmament mutually complement and strengthen each other.

4.   The Disarmament Decade solemnly declared in 1969 by the United Nations is coming to an end. Unfortunately, the objectives established on that occasion by the General Assembly appear to be as far away today as they were then, or even further because the arms race is not diminishing but increasing and outstrips by far the efforts to curb it. While it is true that some limited agreements have been reached, "effective measures relating to the cessation of the nuclear arms race at an early date and to nuclear disarmament" continue to elude man's grasp. Yet the implementation of such measures is urgently required. There has not been any real progress either that might lead to the conclusion of a treaty on general and complete disarmament under effective international control. Furthermore, it has not been possible to free any amount, however modest, of the enormous resources, both material and human, which are wasted on the unproductive and spiralling arms race and which should be made available for the purpose of economic and social development, especially since such a race "places a great burden on both the developing and the developed countries".

5.   The Members of the United Nations are fully aware of the conviction of their peoples that the question of general and complete disarmament is of utmost importance and that peace, security and economic and social development are indivisible, and

they have therefore recognized that the corresponding obligations and responsibilities are universal.

6.   Thus a powerful current of opinion has gradually formed, leading to the convening of what will go down in the annals of the United Nations as the first special session of the General Assembly devoted entirely to disarmament.

7.   The outcome of this special session, whose deliberations have to a large extent been facilitated by the five sessions of the Preparatory Committee which preceded it, is the present Final Document. This introduction serves as a preface to the document which comprises also the following three sections: a Declaration, a Programme of Action and recommendations concerning the international machinery for disarmament negotiations.

8.   While the final objective of the efforts of all States should continue to be general and complete disarmament under effective international control, the immediate goal is that of the elimination of the danger of a nuclear war and the implementation of measures to halt and reverse the arms race and clear the path towards lasting peace. Negotiations on the entire range of those issues should be based on the strict observance of the purposes and principles enshrined in the Charter of the United Nations, with full recognition of the role of the United Nations in the field of disarmament and reflecting the vital interest of all the peoples of the world in this sphere. The aim of the Declaration is to review and assess the existing situation, outline the objectives and the priority tasks and set forth fundamental principles for disarmament negotiations.

9.   For disarmament—the aims and purposes of which the Declaration proclaims—to become a reality, it was essential to agree on a series of specific disarmament measures, selected by common accord as those on which there is a consensus to the effect that their subsequent realization in the short term appears to be feasible. There is also a need to prepare through agreed procedures a comprehensive disarmament programme. That programme, passing through all the necessary stages, should lead to general and complete disarmament under effective international control. Procedures for watching over the fulfilment of the obligations thus assumed had also to be agreed upon. That is the purpose of the Programme of Action.

10.   Although the decisive factor for achieving real measures of disarmament is the "political will" of States, especially of those possessing nuclear weapons, a significant role can also be played by the effective functioning of an appropriate international machinery designed to deal with the problems of disarmament in its various aspects. Consequently, it would be necessary that the two kinds of organs required to that end, the deliberative and the negotiating organs, have the appropriate organization and procedures that would be most conducive to obtaining constructive results. The last section of the Final Document, section IV, has been prepared with that end in view.

II.   Declaration

11.   Mankind today is confronted with an unprecedented threat of self-extinction arising from the massive and competitive accumulation of the most destructive weapons ever produced. Existing arsenals of nuclear weapons alone are more than sufficient to destroy all life on earth. Failure of efforts to halt and reverse the arms race, in particular the nuclear arms race, increases the danger of the proliferation of nuclear weapons. Yet the arms race continues. Military budgets are constantly growing, with enormous consumption of human and material resources. The increase in weapons, especially nuclear weapons, far from helping to strengthen international security, on the contrary weakens it. The vast stockpiles and tremendous build-up of arms and armed forces and the competition for qualitative refinement of weapons of all kinds, to which scientific resources and technological advances are diverted, pose incalculable threats to peace. This situation both reflects and aggravates international tensions, sharpens conflicts in various regions of the world, hinders the process of détente, exacerbates the differences between opposing military alliances, jeopardizes the security of all States, heightens the sense of insecurity among all States, including the non-nuclear-weapon States, and increases the threat of nuclear war.

12.   The arms race, particularly in its nuclear aspect, runs counter to efforts to achieve further relaxation of international tension, to establish international relations based on peaceful coexistence and trust between all States, and to develop broad

international co-operation and understanding. The arms race impedes the realization of the purposes, and is incompatible with the principles, of the Charter of the United Nations, especially respect for sovereignty, refraining from the threat or use of force against the territorial integrity or political independence of any State, the peaceful settlement of disputes and non-intervention and non-interference in the internal affairs of States. It also adversely affects the right of peoples freely to determine their systems of social and economic development, and hinders the struggle for self-determination and the elimination of colonial rule, racial or foreign domination or occupation. Indeed, the massive accumulation of armaments and the acquisition of armaments technology by racist régimes, as well as their possible acquisition of nuclear weapons, present a challenging and increasingly dangerous obstacle to a world community faced with the urgent need to disarm. It is, therefore, essential for purposes of disarmament to prevent any further acquisition of arms or arms technology by such régimes, especially through strict adherence by all States to relevant decisions of the Security Council.

13.   Enduring international peace and security cannot be built on the accumulation of weaponry by military alliances nor be sustained by a precarious balance of deterrence or doctrines of strategic superiority. Genuine and lasting peace can only be created through the effective implementation of the security system provided for in the Charter of the United Nations and the speedy and substantial reduction of arms and armed forces, by international agreement and mutual example, leading ultimately to general and complete disarmament under effective international control. At the same time, the causes of the arms race and threats to peace must be reduced and to this end effective action should be taken to eliminate tensions and settle disputes by peaceful means.

14.   Since the process of disarmament affects the vital security interests of all States, they must all be actively concerned with and contribute to the measures of disarmament and arms limitation, which have an essential part to play in maintaining and strengthening international security. Therefore the role and responsibility of the United Nations in the sphere of disarmament, in accordance with its Charter, must be strengthened.

15.   It is essential that not only Governments but also the peoples of the world recognize and understand the dangers in the present situation. In order that an international conscience may develop and that world public opinion may exercise a positive influence, the United Nations should increase the dissemination of information on the armaments race and disarmament with the full co-operation of Member States.

16.   In a world of finite resources there is a close relationship between expenditure on armaments and economic and social development. Military expenditures are reaching ever higher levels, the highest percentage of which can be attributed to the nuclear-weapon States and most of their allies, with prospects of further expansion and the danger of further increases in the expenditures of other countries. The hundreds of billions of dollars spent annually on the manufacture or improvement of weapons are in sombre and dramatic contrast to the want and poverty in which two thirds of the world's population live. This colossal waste of resources is even more serious in that it diverts to military purposes not only material but also technical and human resources which are urgently needed for development in all countries, particularly in the developing countries. Thus, the economic and social consequences of the arms race are so detrimental that its continuation is obviously incompatible with the implementation of the new international economic order based on justice, equity and co-operation. Consequently, resources released as a result of the implementation of disarmament measures should be used in a manner which will help to promote the well-being of all peoples and to improve the economic conditions of the developing countries.

17.   Disarmament has thus become an imperative and most urgent task facing the international community. No real progress has been made so far in the crucial field of reduction of armaments. However, certain positive changes in international relations in some areas of the world provide some encouragement. Agreements have been reached that have been important in limiting certain weapons or eliminating them altogether, as in the case of the Convention on the Prohibition of the Development, Production and Stockpiling of Bacteriological (Biological) and Toxin Weapons and on Their

Destruction[1] and excluding particular areas from the arms race. The fact remains that these agreements relate only to measures of limited restraint while the arms race continues. These partial measures have done little to bring the world closer to the goal of general and complete disarmament. For more than a decade there have been no negotiations leading to a treaty on general and complete disarmament. The pressing need now is to translate into practical terms the provisions of this Final Document and to proceed along the road of binding and effective international agreements in the field of disarmament.

18. Removing the threat of a world war—a nuclear war—is the most acute and urgent task of the present day. Mankind is confronted with a choice: we must halt the arms race and proceed to disarmament or face annihilation.

19. The ultimate objective of the efforts of States in the disarmament process is general and complete disarmament under effective international control. The principal goals of disarmament are to ensure the survival of mankind and to eliminate the danger of war, in particular nuclear war, to ensure that war is no longer an instrument for settling international disputes and that the use and the threat of force are eliminated from international life, as provided for in the Charter of the United Nations. Progress towards this objective requires the conclusion and implementation of agreements on the cessation of the arms race and on genuine measures of disarmament, taking into account the need of States to protect their security.

20. Among such measures, effective measures of nuclear disarmament and the prevention of nuclear war have the highest priority. To this end, it is imperative to remove the threat of nuclear weapons, to halt and reverse the nuclear arms race until the total elimination of nuclear weapons and their delivery systems has been achieved, and to prevent the proliferation of nuclear weapons. At the same time, other measures designed to prevent the outbreak of nuclear war and to lessen the danger of the threat or use of nuclear weapons should be taken.

---

[1] Resolution 2826 (XXVI), annex.

21.   Along with these measures, agreements or other effective measures should be adopted to prohibit or prevent the development, production or use of other weapons of mass destruction. In this context, an agreement on elimination of all chemical weapons should be concluded as a matter of high priority.

22.   Together with negotiations on nuclear disarmament measures, negotiations should be carried out on the balanced reduction of armed forces and of conventional armaments, based on the principle of undiminished security of the parties with a view to promoting or enhancing stability at a lower military level, taking into account the need of all States to protect their security. These negotiations should be conducted with particular emphasis on armed forces and conventional weapons of nuclear-weapon States and other militarily significant countries. There should also be negotiations on the limitation of international transfer of conventional weapons, based in particular on the same principle, and taking into account: the inalienable right to self-determination and independence of peoples under colonial or foreign domination and the obligations of States to respect that right, in accordance with the Charter of the United Nations and the Declaration on Principles of International Law concerning Friendly Relations and Co-operation among States,[2] as well as the need of recipient States to protect their security.

23.   Further international action should be taken to prohibit or restrict for humanitarian reasons the use of specific conventional weapons, including those which may be excessively injurious, cause unnecessary suffering or have indiscriminate effects.

24.   Collateral measures in both the nuclear and conventional fields, together with other measures specifically designed to build confidence, should be undertaken in order to contribute to the creation of favourable conditions for the adoption of additional disarmament measures and to further the relaxation of international tension.

25.   Negotiations and measures in the field of disarmament shall be guided by the fundamental principles set forth below.

---

[2] Resolution 2625 (XXV), annex.

26.   All States Members of the United Nations reaffirm their full commitment to the purposes of the Charter of the United Nations and their obligation strictly to observe its principles as well as other relevant and generally accepted principles of international law relating to the maintenance of international peace and security. They stress the special importance of refraining from the threat or use of force against the sovereignty, territorial integrity or political independence of any State, or against peoples under colonial or foreign domination seeking to exercise their right to self-determination and to achieve independence; non-intervention and non-interference in the internal affairs of other States; the inviolability of international frontiers; and the peaceful settlement of disputes, having regard to the inherent right of States to individual and collective self-defence in accordance with the Charter.

27.   In accordance with the Charter, the United Nations has a central role and primary responsibility in the sphere of disarmament. In order effectively to discharge this role and facilitate and encourage all measures in this field, the United Nations should be kept appropriately informed of all steps in this field, whether unilateral, bilateral, regional or multilateral, without prejudice to the progress of negotiations.

28.   All the peoples of the world have a vital interest in the success of disarmament negotiations. Consequently, all States have the duty to contribute to efforts in the field of disarmament. All States have the right to participate in disarmament negotiations. They have the right to participate on an equal footing in those multilateral disarmament negotiations which have a direct bearing on their national security. While disarmament is the responsibility of all States, the nuclear-weapons States have the primary responsibility for nuclear disarmament and, together with other militarily significant States, for halting and reversing the arms race. It is therefore important to secure their active participation.

29.   The adoption of disarmament measures should take place in such an equitable and balanced manner as to ensure the right of each State to security and to ensure that no individual State or group of States may obtain advantages over others at any stage.

At each stage the objective should be undiminished security at the lowest possible level of armaments and military forces.

30. An acceptable balance of mutual responsibilities and obligations for nuclear and non-nuclear-weapon State should be strictly observed.

31. Disarmament and arms limitation agreements should provide for adequate measures of verification satisfactory to all parties concerned in order to create the necessary confidence and ensure that they are being observed by all parties. The form and modalities of the verification to be provided for in any specific agreement depend upon and should be determined by the purposes, scope and nature of the agreement. Agreements should provide for participation of parties directly or through the United Nations system in the verification process. Where appropriate, a combination of several methods of verification as well as other compliance procedures should be employed.

32. All States, in particular nuclear-weapon States, should consider various proposals designed to secure the avoidance of the use of nuclear weapons, and the prevention of nuclear war. In this context, while noting the declarations made by nuclear-weapon States, effective arrangements, as appropriate, to assure non-nuclear-weapon States against the use or the threat of use of nuclear weapons could strengthen the security of those States and international peace and security.

33. The establishment of nuclear-weapon-free zones on the basis of agreements or arrangements freely arrived at among the States of the zone concerned and the full compliance with those agreements or arrangements, thus ensuring that the zones are genuinely free from nuclear weapons, and respect for such zones by nuclear-weapon States constitute an important disarmament measure.

34. Disarmament, relaxation of international tension, respect for the right to self-determination and national independence, the peaceful settlement of disputes in accordance with the Charter of the United Nations and the strengthening of international peace and security are directly related to each other. Progress in any of these spheres has a beneficial effect on all of them; in turn, failure in one sphere has negative effects on others.

35.   There is also a close relationship between disarmament and development. Progress in the former would help greatly in the realization of the latter. Therefore resources released as a result of the implementation of disarmament measures should be devoted to the economic and social development of all nations and contribute to the bridging of the economic gap between developed and developing countries.

36.   Non-proliferation of nuclear weapons is a matter of universal concern. Measures of disarmament must be consistent with the inalienable right of all States, without discrimination, to develop, acquire and use nuclear technology, equipment and materials for the peaceful use of nuclear energy and to determine their peaceful nuclear programmes in accordance with their national priorities, needs and interests, bearing in mind the need to prevent the proliferation of nuclear weapons. International co-operation in the peaceful uses of nuclear energy should be conducted under agreed and appropriate international safeguards applied on a non-discriminatory basis.

37.   Significant progress in disarmament, including nuclear disarmament, would be facilitated by parallel measures to strengthen the security of States and to improve the international situation in general.

38.   Negotiations on partial measures of disarmament should be conducted concurrently with negotiations on more comprehensive measures and should be followed by negotiations leading to a treaty on general and complete disarmament under effective international control.

39.   Qualitative and quantitative disarmament measures are both important for halting the arms race. Efforts to that end must include negotiations on the limitation and cessation of the qualitative improvement of armaments, especially weapons of mass destruction and the development of new means of warfare so that ultimately scientific and technological achievements may be used solely for peaceful purposes.

40.   Universality of disarmament agreements helps create confidence among States. When multilateral agreements in the field of disarmament are negotiated, every effort should be made to

ensure that they are universally acceptable. The full compliance of all parties with the provisions contained in such agreements would also contribute to the attainment of that goal.

41.   In order to create favourable conditions for success in the disarmament process, all States should strictly abide by the provisions of the Charter of the United Nations, refrain from actions which might adversely affect efforts in the field of disarmament, and display a constructive approach to negotiations and the political will to reach agreements. There are certain negotiations on disarmament under way at different levels, the early and successful completion of which could contribute to limiting the arms race. Unilateral measures of arms limitation or reduction could also contribute to the attainment of that goal.

42.   Since prompt measures should be taken in order to halt and reverse the arms race, Member States hereby declare that they will respect the objectives and principles stated above and make every effort faithfully to carry out the Programme of Action set forth in section III below.

III.   Programme of Action

43.   Progress towards the goal of general and complete disarmament can be achieved through the implementation of a programme of action on disarmament, in accordance with the goals and principles established in the Declaration on disarmament. The present Programme of Action contains priorities and measures in the field of disarmament that States should undertake as a matter of urgency with a view to halting and reversing the arms race and to giving the necessary impetus to efforts designed to achieve genuine disarmament leading to general and complete disarmament under effective international control.

44.   The present Programme of Action enumerates the specific measures of disarmament which should be implemented over the next few years, as well as other measures and studies to prepare the way for future negotiations and for progress towards general and complete disarmament.

45.   Priorities in disarmament negotiations shall be: nuclear weapons; other weapons of mass destruction, including chemical

weapons; conventional weapons, including any which may be deemed to be excessively injurious or to have indiscriminate effects; and reduction of armed forces.

46.   Nothing should preclude States from conducting negotiations on all priority items concurrently.

47.   Nuclear weapons pose the greatest danger to mankind and to the survival of civilization. It is essential to halt and reverse the nuclear arms race in all its aspects in order to avert the danger of war involving nuclear weapons. The ultimate goal in this context is the complete elimination of nuclear weapons.

48.   In the task of achieving the goals of nuclear disarmament, all the nuclear-weapon States, in particular those among them which possess the most important nuclear arsenals, bear a special responsibility.

49.   The process of nuclear disarmament should be carried out in such a way, and requires measures to ensure, that the security of all States is guaranteed at progressively lower levels of nuclear armaments, taking into account the relative qualitative and quantitative importance of the existing arsenals of the nuclear-weapon States and other States concerned.

50.   The achievement of nuclear disarmament will require urgent negotiation of agreements at appropriate stages and with adequate measures of verification satisfactory to the States concerned for:

(a)   Cessation of the qualitative improvement and development of nuclear-weapon systems;

(b)   Cessation of the production of all types of nuclear weapons and their means of delivery, and of the production of fissionable material for weapons purposes;

(c)   A comprehensive, phased programme with agreed time-frames, whenever feasible, for progressive and balanced reduction of stockpiles of nuclear weapons and their means of delivery, leading to their ultimate and complete elimination at the earliest possible time.

Consideration can be given in the course of the negotiations to mutual and agreed limitation or prohibition, without prejudice to the security of any State, of any types of nuclear armaments.

51. The cessation of nuclear-weapon testing by all States within the framework of an effective nuclear disarmament process would be in the interest of mankind. It would make a significant contribution to the above aim of ending the qualitative improvement of nuclear weapons and the development of new types of such weapons and of preventing the proliferation of nuclear weapons. In this context the negotiations now in progress on "a treaty prohibiting nuclear-weapon tests, and a protocol covering nuclear explosions for peaceful purposes, which would be an integral part of the treaty," should be concluded urgently and the result submitted for full consideration by the multilateral negotiating body with a view to the submission of a draft treaty to the General Assembly at the earliest possible date. All efforts should be made by the negotiating parties to achieve an agreements which, following endorsement by the General Assembly, could attract the widest possible adherence. In this context, various views were expressed by non-nuclear-weapon States that, pending the conclusion of this treaty, the world community would be encouraged if all the nuclear-weapon States refrained from testing nuclear weapons. In this connexion, some nuclear-weapon States expressed different views.

52. The Union of Soviet Socialist Republics and the United States of America should conclude at the earliest possible date the agreement they have been pursuing for several years in the second series of the strategic arms limitation talks. They are invited to transmit in good time the text of the agreement to the General Assembly. It should be followed promptly by further strategic arms limitation negotiations between the two parties, leading to agreed significant reductions of, and qualitative limitations on, strategic arms. It should constitute an important step in the direction of nuclear disarmament and, ultimately, of establishment of a world free of such weapons.

53. The process of nuclear disarmament described in the paragraph on this subject should be expedited by the urgent and vigorous pursuit to a successful conclusion of ongoing negotiations and the urgent initiation of further negotiations among the nuclear-weapon States.

54.   Significant progress in nuclear disarmament would be facilitated both by parallel political or international legal measures to strengthen the security of States and by progress in the limitation and reduction of armed forces and conventional armaments of the nuclear-weapon States and other States in the regions concerned.

55.   Real progress in the field of nuclear disarmament could create an atmosphere conducive to progress in conventional disarmament on a world-wide basis.

56.   The most effective guarantee against the danger of nuclear war and the use of nuclear weapons is nuclear disarmament and the complete elimination of nuclear weapons.

57.   Pending the achievement of this goal, for which negotiations should be vigorously pursued, and bearing in mind the devastating results which nuclear war would have on belligerents and non-belligerents alike, the nuclear-weapon States have special responsibilities to undertake measures aimed at preventing the outbreak of nuclear war, and of the use of force in international relations, subject to the provisions of the Charter of the United Nations, including the use of nuclear weapons.

58.   In this context all States, in particular nuclear-weapon States, should consider as soon as possible various proposals designed to secure the avoidance of the use of nuclear weapons, the prevention of nuclear war and related objectives, where possible through international agreement, and thereby ensure that the survival of mankind is not endangered. All States should actively participate in efforts to bring about conditions in international relations among States in which a code of peaceful conduct of nations in international affairs could be agreed and which would preclude the use or threat of use of nuclear weapons.

59.   In the same context, the nuclear-weapon States are called upon to take steps to assure the non-nuclear-weapon States against the use or threat of use of nuclear weapons. The General Assembly notes the declarations made by the nuclear-weapon States and urges them to pursue efforts to conclude, as appropriate, effective arrangements to assure non-nuclear-weapon States against the use or threat of use of nuclear weapons.

60.   The establishment of nuclear-weapon-free zones on the basis of arrangements freely arrived at among the States of the region concerned constitutes an important disarmament measure.

61.   The process of establishing such zones in different parts of the world should be encouraged with the ultimate objective of achieving a world entirely free of nuclear weapons. In the process of establishing such zones, the characteristics of each region should be taken into account. The States participating in such zones should undertake to comply fully with all the objectives, purposes and principles of the agreements or arrangements establishing the zones, thus ensuring that they are genuinely free from nuclear weapons.

62.   With respect to such zones, the nuclear-weapon States in turn are called upon to give undertakings, the modalities of which are to be negotiated with the competent authority of each zone, in particular:

(a)   To respect strictly the status of the nuclear-weapon-free zone;

(b)   To refrain from the use or threat of use of nuclear weapons against the States of the zone.

63.   In the light of existing conditions, and without prejudice to other measures which may be considered in other regions, the following measures are especially desirable:

(a)   Adoption by the States concerned of all relevant measures to ensure the full application of the Treaty for the Prohibition of Nuclear Weapons in Latin America (Treaty of Tlatelolco),[3] taking into account the views expressed at the tenth special session on the adherence to it;

(b)   Signature and ratification of the Additional Protocols of the Treaty for the Prohibition of Nuclear Weapons in Latin America (Treaty of Tlatelolco) by the States entitled to become parties to those instruments which have not yet done so;

(c)   In Africa, where the Organization of African Unity has affirmed a decision for the denuclearization of the region,

---

[3] United Nations, Treaty Series, vol. 634, No. 9068.

the Security Council of the United Nations shall take appropriate effective steps whenever necessary to prevent the frustration of this objective;

(d)   The serious consideration of the practical and urgent steps, as described in the paragraphs above, required for the implementation of the proposal to establish a nuclear-weapon-free zone in the Middle East, in accordance with the relevant General Assembly resolutions, where all parties directly concerned have expressed their support for the concept and where the danger of nuclear-weapon proliferation exists. The establishment of a nuclear-weapon-free zone in the Middle East would greatly enhance international peace and security. Pending the establishment of such a zone in the region, States of the region should solemnly declare that they will refrain on a reciprocal basis from producing, acquiring or in any other way possessing nuclear weapons and nuclear explosive devices and from permitting the stationing of nuclear weapons on their territory by any third party, and agree to place all their nuclear activities under International Atomic Energy Agency safeguards. Consideration should be given to a Security Council role in advancing the establishment of a nuclear-weapon-free zone in the Middle East;

(e)   All States in the region of South Asia have expressed their determination to keep their countries free of nuclear weapons. No action should be taken by them which might deviate from that objective. In this context, the question of establishing a nuclear-weapon-free zone in South Asia has been dealt with in several resolutions of the General Assembly, which is keeping the subject under consideration.

64.   The establishment of zones of peace in various regions of the world under appropriate conditions, to be clearly defined and determined freely by the States concerned in the zone, taking into account the characteristics of the zone and the principles of the Charter of the United Nations, and in conformity with international law, can contribute to strengthening the security of States within such zones and to international peace and security as a whole. In this regard, the General Assembly notes the proposals for the establishment of zones of peace, *inter alia*, in:

(a)   South-East Asia where States in the region have expressed interest in the establishment of such a zone, in conformity with their views;

(b)   The Indian Ocean, taking into account the deliberations of the General Assembly and its relevant resolutions and the need to ensure the maintenance of peace and security in the region.

65.   It is imperative, as an integral part of the effort to halt and reverse the arms race, to prevent the proliferation of nuclear weapons. The goal of nuclear non-proliferation is on the one hand to prevent the emergence of any additional nuclear-weapon States besides the existing five nuclear-weapon States, and on the other progressively to reduce and eventually eliminate nuclear weapons altogether. This involves obligations and responsibilities on the part of both nuclear-weapon States and non-nuclear-weapon States, the former undertaking to stop the nuclear arms race and to achieve nuclear disarmament by urgent application of the measures outlined in the relevant paragraphs of this Final Document, and all States undertaking to prevent the spread of nuclear weapons.

66.   Effective measures can and should be taken at the national level and through international agreements to minimize the danger of the proliferation of nuclear weapons without jeopardizing energy supplies or the development of nuclear energy for peaceful purposes. Therefore, the nuclear-weapon States and the non-nuclear-weapon States should jointly take further steps to develop an international consensus of ways and means, on a universal and non-discriminatory basis, to prevent the proliferation of nuclear weapons.

67.   Full implementation of all the provisions of existing instruments on non-proliferation, such as the Treaty on the Non-Proliferation of Nuclear Weapons[4] and/or the Treaty for the Prohibition of Nuclear Weapons in Latin America (Treaty of Tlatelolco) by States parties to those instruments will be an important contribution to this end. Adherence to such instruments has increased in recent years and the hope has been expressed by the parties that this trend might continue.

---

[4] Resolution 2373 (XXII), annex.

68. Non-proliferation measures should not jeopardize the full exercise of the inalienable rights of all States to apply and develop their programmes for the peaceful uses of nuclear energy for economic and social development in conformity with their priorities, interests and needs. All States should also have access to and be free to acquire technology, equipment and materials for peaceful uses of nuclear energy, taking into account the particular needs of the developing countries. International co-operation in this field should be under agreed and appropriate international safeguards applied through the International Atomic Energy Agency on a non-discriminatory basis in order to prevent effectively the proliferation of nuclear weapons.

69. Each country's choices and decisions in the field of the peaceful uses of nuclear energy should be respected without jeopardizing their respective fuel cycle policies or international co-operation, agreements and contracts for the peaceful uses of nuclear energy, provided that the agreed safeguard measures mentioned above are applied.

70. In accordance with the principles and provisions of the General Assembly resolution 32/50 of 8 December 1977, international co-operation for the promotion of the transfer and utilization of nuclear technology for economic and social development, especially in the developing countries, should be strengthened.

71. Efforts should be made to conclude the work of the International Nuclear Fuel Cycle Evaluation strictly in accordance with the objectives set out in the final communiqué of its Organizing Conference.[5]

72. All States should adhere to the Protocol for the Prohibition of the Use in War of Asphyxiating, Poisonous or Other Gases, and of Bacteriological Methods of Warfare, signed at Geneva on 17 June 1925.[6]

73. All States which have not yet done so should consider adhering to the Convention on the Prohibition of the Development,

---

[5] See A/C.1/32/7.
[6] League of Nations, Treaty Series, vol. XCIV (1929), No. 2138.

Production and Stockpiling of Bacteriological (Biological) and Toxin Weapons and on Their Destruction.

74.   States should also consider the possibility of adhering to multilateral agreements concluded so far in the disarmament field which are mentioned below in this section.

75.   The complete and effective prohibition of the development, production and stockpiling of all chemical weapons and their destruction represent one of the most urgent measures of disarmament. Consequently, the conclusion of a convention to this end, on which negotiations have been going on for several years, is one of the most urgent tasks of multilateral negotiations. After its conclusion, all States should contribute to ensuring the broadest possible application of the convention through its early signature and ratification.

76.   A convention should be concluded prohibiting the development, production, stockpiling and use of radiological weapons.

77.   In order to help prevent a qualitative arms race and so that scientific and technological achievements may ultimately be used solely for peaceful purposes, effective measures should be taken to avoid the danger and prevent the emergence of new types of weapons of mass destruction based on new scientific principles and achievements. Efforts should be appropriately pursued aiming at the prohibition of such new types and new systems of weapons of mass destruction. Specific agreements could be concluded on particular types of new weapons of mass destruction which may be identified. This question should be kept under continuing review.

78.   The Committee on Disarmament should keep under review the need for a further prohibition of military or any other hostile use of environmental modification techniques in order to eliminate the dangers to mankind from such use.

79.   In order to promote the peaceful use of and to avoid an arms race on the sea-bed and the ocean floor and the subsoil thereof, the Committee on Disarmament is requested—in consultation with the States parties to the Treaty on the Prohibition of the Emplacement of Nuclear Weapons and Other Weapons of Mass Destruction on

the Sea-Bed and the Ocean Floor and in the Subsoil Thereof,[7] and taking into account the proposals made during the 1977 Review Conference of the parties to that Treaty and any relevant technological developments—to proceed promptly with the consideration of further measures in the field of disarmament for the prevention of an arms race in that environment.

80.   In order to prevent an arms race in outer space, further measures should be taken and appropriate international negotiations held in accordance with the spirit of the Treaty on Principles Governing the Activities of States in the Exploration and Use of Outer Space, including the Moon and Other Celestial Bodies.[8]

81.   Together with negotiations on nuclear disarmament measures, the limitation and gradual reduction of armed forces and conventional weapons should be resolutely pursued within the framework of progress towards general and complete disarmament. States with the largest military arsenals have a special responsibility in pursuing the process of conventional armaments reductions.

82.   In particular the achievement of a more stable situation in Europe at a lower level of military potential on the basis of approximate equality and parity, as well as on the basis of undiminished security of all States with full respect for security interests and independence of States outside military alliances, by agreement on appropriate mutual reductions and limitations would contribute to the strengthening of security in Europe and constitute a significant step towards enhancing international peace and security. Current efforts to this end should be continued most energetically.

83.   Agreements or other measures should be resolutely pursued on a bilateral, regional and multilateral basis with the aim of strengthening peace and security at a lower level of forces, by the limitation and reduction of armed forces and of conventional weapons, taking into account the need of States to protect their security, bearing in mind the inherent right of self-defence embodied in the Charter of the United Nations and without prejudice to the principle of equal rights and self-determination

---

[7] Resolution 2660 (XXV), annex.
[8] Resolution 2222 (XXI), annex.

of peoples in accordance with the Charter, and the need to ensure balance at each stage and undiminished security of all States. Such measures might include those in the following two paragraphs.

84.   Bilateral,   regional   and   multilateral   consultations   and conferences should be held where appropriate conditions exist with the participation of all the countries concerned for the consideration of different aspects of conventional disarmament, such as the initiative envisaged in the Declaration of Ayacucho subscribed to by eight Latin American countries on 9 December 1974.[9]

85.   Consultations   should   be   carried   out   among   major   arms supplier and recipient countries on the limitation of all types of international transfer of conventional weapons, based in particular on the principle of undiminished security of the parties with a view to promoting or enhancing stability at a lower military level, taking into account the need of all States to protect their security as well as the inalienable right to self-determination and independence of peoples under colonial or foreign domination and the obligations of States to respect that right, in accordance with the Charter of the United Nations and the Declaration on Principles of International Law concerning Friendly Relations and Co-operation among States.

86.   The   United   Nations   Conference   on   Prohibitions   or Restrictions of Use of Certain Conventional Weapons Which May be Deemed to Be Excessively Injurious or to Have Indiscriminate Effects, to be held in 1979, should seek agreement, in the light of humanitarian and military considerations, on the prohibition or restriction of use of certain conventional weapons including those which may cause unnecessary suffering or have indiscriminate effects. The Conference should consider specific categories of such weapons, including those which were the subject-matter of previously conducted discussions.

87.   All States are called upon to contribute towards carrying out this task.

88.   The result of the Conference should be considered by all States, especially producer States, in regard to the question of the transfer of such weapons to other States.

---

[9]   See A/10044, annex.

89.   Gradual reduction of military budgets on a mutually agreed basis, for example, in absolute figures or in terms of percentage points, particularly by nuclear-weapon States and other militarily significant States, would be a measure that would contribute to the curbing of the arms race and would increase the possibilities of reallocation of resources now being used for military purposes to economic and social development, particularly for the benefit of the developing countries. The basis for implementing this measure will have to be agreed by all participating States and will require ways and means of its implementation acceptable to all of them, taking account of the problems involved in assessing the relative significance of reductions as among different States and with due regard to the proposals of States on all the aspects of reduction of military budgets.

90.   The General Assembly should continue to consider what concrete steps should be taken to facilitate the reduction of military budgets, bearing in mind the relevant proposals and documents of the United Nations on this question.

91.   In order to facilitate the conclusion and effective implementation of disarmament agreements and to create confidence, States should accept appropriate provisions for verification in such agreements.

92.   in the context of international disarmament negotiations, the problem of verification should be further examined and adequate methods and procedures in this field be considered. Every effort should be made to develop appropriate methods and procedures which are non-discriminatory and which do not unduly interfere with the internal affairs of other States or jeopardize their economic and social development.

93.   In order to facilitate the process of disarmament, it is necessary to take measures and pursue policies to strengthen international peace and security and to build confidence among States. Commitment to confidence-building measures could significantly contribute to preparing for further progress in disarmament. For this purpose, measures such as the following, and other measures yet to be agreed upon, should be undertaken:

(a)   The prevention of attacks which take place by accident, miscalculation or communications failure by taking steps to improve communications between Governments, particularly in areas of tension, by the establishment of "hot lines" and other methods of reducing the risk of conflict;

(b)   States should assess the possible implications of their military research and development for existing agreements as well as for further efforts in the field of disarmament;

(c)   The Secretary-General shall periodically submit reports to the General Assembly on the economic and social consequences of the armaments race and its extremely harmful effects on world peace and security.

94.   In view of the relationship between expenditure on armaments and economic and social development and the necessity to release real resources now being used for military purposes to economic and social development in the world, particularly for the benefit of the developing countries, the Secretary-General should, with the assistance of a group of qualified governmental experts appointed by him, initiate an expert study on the relationship between disarmament and development. The Secretary-General should submit an interim report on the subject to the General Assembly at its thirty-fourth session and submit the final results to the Assembly at its thirty-sixth session for subsequent action.

95.   The expert study should have the terms of reference contained in the report of the *Ad Hoc* Group on the Relationship between Disarmament and Development[10] appointed by the Secretary-General in accordance with General Assembly resolution 32/88 A of 12 December 1977. It should investigate the three main areas listed in the report, bearing in mind the United Nations studies previously carried out. The study should be made in the context of how disarmament can contribute to the establishment of the new international economic order. The study should be forward-looking and policy-oriented and place special emphasis on both the desirability of a reallocation, following disarmament measures, of resources now being used for military purposes to economic and social development, particularly for the benefit of the developing

---

[10] A/S-10/9, annex.

countries, and the substantive feasibility of such a reallocation. A principal aim should be to produce results that could effectively guide the formulation of practical measures to reallocate those resources at the local, national, regional and international levels.

96. Taking further steps in the field of disarmament and other measures aimed at promoting international peace and security would be facilitated by carrying out studies by the Secretary-General in this field with appropriate assistance from governmental or consultant experts.

97. The Secretary-General shall, with the assistance of consultant experts appointed by him, continue the study of the interrelationship between disarmament and international security requested in Assembly resolution 32/87 C of 12 December 1977 and submit it to the thirty-fourth session of the General Assembly.

98. At its thirty-third and subsequent sessions the General Assembly should determine the specific guidelines for carrying out studies, taking into account the proposals already submitted including those made by individual countries at the special session, as well as other proposals which can be introduced later in this field. In doing so, the Assembly would take into consideration a report on these matters prepared by the Secretary-General.

99. In order to mobilize world public opinion on behalf of disarmament, the specific measures set forth below, designed to increase the dissemination of information about the armaments race and the efforts to halt and reverse it, should be adopted.

100. Governmental and non-governmental information organs and those of the United Nations and its specialized agencies should give priority to the preparation and distribution of printed and audio-visual material relating to the danger represented by the armaments race as well as to the disarmament efforts and negotiations on specific disarmament measures.

101. In particular, publicity should be given to the Final Document of the tenth special session.

102. The General Assembly proclaims the week starting 24 October, the day of the foundation of the United Nations, as a week devoted to fostering the objectives of disarmament.

103. To encourage study and research on disarmament, the United Nations Centre for Disarmament should intensify its activities in the presentation of information concerning the armaments race and disarmament. Also, the United Nations Educational, Scientific and Cultural Organization is urged to intensify its activities aimed at facilitating research and publications on disarmament, related to its fields of competence, especially in developing countries, and should disseminate the results of such research.

104. Throughout this process of disseminating information about developments in the disarmament field of all countries, there should be increased participation by non-governmental organizations concerned with the matter, through closer liaison between them and the United Nations.

105. Member States should be encouraged to ensure a better flow of information with regard to the various aspects of disarmament to avoid dissemination of false and tendentious information concerning armaments, and to concentrate on the danger of escalation of the armaments race and on the need for general and complete disarmament under effective international control.

106. With a view to contributing to a greater understanding and awareness of the problems created by the armaments race and of the need for disarmament, Governments and governmental and non-governmental international organizations are urged to take steps to develop programmes of education for disarmament and peace studies at all levels.

107. The General Assembly welcomes the initiative or the United Nations Educational, Scientific and Cultural Organization in planning to hold a world congress on disarmament education and, in this connexion, urges that organization to step up its programme aimed at the development of disarmament education as a distinct field of study through the preparation, *inter alia*, of teachers' guides, textbooks, readers and audio-visual materials. Member States should take all possible measures to encourage the incorporation of such materials in the curricula of their educational institutes.

108. In order to promote expertise in disarmament in more Member States, particularly in the developing countries, the

General Assembly decides to establish a programme of fellowships on disarmament. The Secretary-General, taking into account the proposal submitted to the special session, should prepare guidelines for the programme. He should also submit the financial requirements of twenty fellowships to the General Assembly at its thirty-third session for inclusion in the regular budget of the United Nations, bearing in mind the savings that can be made within the existing budgetary appropriations.

109. Implementation of these priorities should lead to general and complete disarmament under effective international control, which remains the ultimate goal of all efforts exerted in the field of disarmament. Negotiations on general and complete disarmament shall be conducted concurrently with negotiations on partial measures of disarmament. With this purpose in mind, the Committee on Disarmament will undertake the elaboration of a comprehensive programme of disarmament encompassing all measures thought to be advisable in order to ensure that the goal of general and complete disarmament under effective international control becomes a reality in a world in which international peace and security prevail and in which the new international economic order is strengthened and consolidated. The comprehensive programme should contain appropriate procedures for ensuring that the General Assembly is kept fully informed of the progress of the negotiations including an appraisal of the situation when appropriate and, in particular, a continuing review of the implementation of the programme.

110. Progress in disarmament should be accompanied by measures to strengthen institutions for maintaining peace and the settlement of international disputes by peaceful means. During and after the implementation of the programme of general and complete disarmament, there should be taken, in accordance with the principles of the Charter of the United Nations, the necessary measures to maintain international peace and security, including the obligation of States to place at the disposal of the United Nations agreed manpower necessary for an international peace force to be equipped with agreed types of armaments. Arrangements for the use of this force should ensure that the United Nations can effectively deter or supress any threat or use of arms in violation of the purposes and principles of the United Nations.

111. General and complete disarmament under strict and effective international control shall permit States to have at their disposal only those non-nuclear forces, armaments, facilities and establishments as are agreed to be necessary to maintain internal order and protect the personal security of citizens and in order that States shall support and provide agreed manpower for a United Nations peace force.

112. In addition to the several questions dealt with in this Programme of Action, there are a few others of fundamental importance, on which, because of the complexity of the issues involved and the short time at the disposal of the special session, it has proved impossible to reach satisfactory agreed conclusions. For those reasons they are treated only in very general terms and, in a few instances, not even treated at all in the Programme. It should be stressed, however, that a number of concrete approaches to deal with such questions emerged from the exchange of views carried out in the General Assembly which will undoubtedly facilitate the continuation of the study and negotiation of the problems involved in the competent disarmament organs.

IV. Machinery

113. While disarmament, particularly in the nuclear field, has become a necessity for the survival of mankind and for the elimination of the danger of nuclear war, little progress has been made since the end of the Second World War. In addition to the need to exercise political will, the international machinery should be utilized more effectively and also improved to enable implementation of the Programme of Action and help the United Nations to fulfil its role in the field of disarmament. In spite of the best efforts of the international community, adequate results have not been produced with the existing machinery. There is, therefore, an urgent need that existing disarmament machinery be revitalized and forums appropriately constituted for disarmament deliberations and negotiations with a better representative character. For maximum effectiveness, two kinds of bodies are required in the field of disarmament—deliberative and negotiating. All Member States should be represented on the former, whereas the latter, for the sake of convenience, should have a relatively small membership.

114. The United Nations, in accordance with the Charter, has a central role and primary responsibility in the sphere of disarmament. Accordingly, it should play a more active role in this field and, in order to discharge its functions effectively, the United Nations should facilitate and encourage all disarmament measures—unilateral, bilateral, regional or multilateral—and be kept duly informed through the General Assembly, or any other appropriate United Nations channel reaching all Members of the Organization, of all disarmament efforts outside its aegis without prejudice to the progress of negotiations.

115. The General Assembly has been and should remain the main deliberative organ of the United Nations in the field of disarmament and should make every effort to facilitate the implementation of disarmament measures. An item entitled "Review of the implementation of the recommendations and decisions adopted by the General Assembly at its tenth special session" shall be included in the provisional agenda of the thirty-third and subsequent sessions of the General Assembly.

116. Draft multilateral disarmament conventions should be subjected to the normal procedures applicable in the law of treaties. Those submitted to the General Assembly for its commendation should be subject to full review by the Assembly.

117. The First Committee of the General Assembly should deal in the future only with questions of disarmament and related international security questions.

118. The General Assembly establishes, as successor to the Commission originally established by resolution 502 (VI) of 11 January 1952, a Disarmament Commission, composed of all States Members of the United Nations, and decides that:

(a) The Disarmament Commission shall be a deliberative body, a subsidiary organ of the General Assembly, the function of which shall be to consider and make recommendations on various problems in the field of disarmament and to follow up the relevant decisions and recommendations of the special session devoted to disarmament. The Disarmament Commission should, *inter alia*, consider the elements of a comprehensive programme for disarmament to be submitted as recommendations to the General

Assembly and, through it, to the negotiating body, the Committee on Disarmament;

(b) The Disarmament Commission shall function under the rules of procedure relating to the committees of the General Assembly with such modifications as the Commission may deem necessary and shall make every effort to ensure that, in so far as possible, decisions on substantive issues be adopted by consensus;

(c) The Disarmament Commission shall report annually to the General Assembly and will submit for consideration by the Assembly at its thirty-third session a report on organizational matters; in 1979, the Disarmament Commission will meet for a period not exceeding four weeks, the dates to be decided at the thirty-third session of the Assembly;

(d) The Secretary-General shall furnish such experts, staff and services as are necessary for the effective accomplishment of the Commission's functions.

119. A second special session of the General Assembly devoted to disarmament should be held on a date to be decided by the Assembly at its thirty-third session.

120. The General Assembly is conscious of the work that has been done by the international negotiating body that has been meeting since 14 March 1962 as well as the considerable and urgent work that remains to be accomplished in the field of disarmament. The Assembly is deeply aware of the continuing requirement for a single multilateral disarmament negotiating forum of limited size taking decisions on the basis of consensus. It attaches great importance to the participation of all the nuclear-weapon States in an appropriately constituted negotiating body, the Committee on Disarmament. The Assembly welcomes the agreement reached following appropriate consultations among the Member States during the special session of the General Assembly devoted to disarmament that the Committee on Disarmament will be open to the nuclear-weapon States, and thirty-two to thirty-five other States to be chosen in consultation with the President of the thirty-second session of the Assembly; that the membership of the Committee on Disarmament will be reviewed at regular intervals; that the Committee on Disarmament will be convened in Geneva not

later than January 1979 by the country whose name appears first in the alphabetical list of membership; and that the Committee on Disarmament will:

(a)   Conduct its work by consensus;

(b)   Adopt its own rules of procedure;

(c)   Request the Secretary-General of the United Nations, following consultations with the Committee on Disarmament, to appoint the Secretary of the Committee, who shall also act as his personal representative, to assist the Committee and its Chairman in organizing the business and time-tables of the Committee;

(d)   Rotate the chairmanship of the Committee among all its members on a monthly basis;

(e)   Adopt its own agenda taking into account the recommendations made to it by the General Assembly and the proposals presented by the members of the Committee;

(f)   Submit a report to the General Assembly annually, or more frequently as appropriate, and provide its formal and other relevant documents to the States Members of the United Nations on a regular basis;

(g)   Make arrangements for interested States, not members of the Committee, to submit to the Committee written proposals or working documents on measures of disarmament that are the subject of negotiation in the Committee and to participate in the discussion of the subject-matter of such proposals or working documents;

(h)   Invite States not members of the Committee, upon their request, to express views in the Committee when the particular concerns of those States are under discussion;

(i)   Open its plenary meetings to the public unless otherwise decided.

121. Bilateral and regional disarmament negotiations may also play an important role and could facilitate negotiations of multilateral agreements in the field of disarmament.

122. At the earliest appropriate time, a world disarmament conference should be convened with universal participation and with adequate preparation.

123. In order to enable the United Nations to continue to fulfil its role in the field of disarmament and to carry out the additional tasks assigned to it by this special session, the United Nations Centre for Disarmament should be adequately strengthened and its research and information functions accordingly extended. The Centre should also take account fully of the possibilities offered by specialized agencies and other institutions and programmes within the United Nations system with regard to studies and information on disarmament. The Centre should also increase contacts with non-governmental organizations and research institutions in view of the valuable role they play in the field of disarmament. This role could be encouraged also in other ways that may be considered as appropriate.

124. The Secretary-General is requested to set up an advisory board of eminent persons, selected on the basis of their personal expertise and taking into account the principle of equitable geographical representation, to advise him on various aspects of studies to be made under the auspices of the United Nations in the field of disarmament and arms limitation, including a programme of such studies.

* * *

125. The General Assembly notes with satisfaction that the active participation of the Member States in the consideration of the agenda items of the special session and the proposals and suggestions submitted by them and reflected to a considerable extent in the Final Document have made a valuable contribution to the work of the special session and to its positive conclusion. Since a number of those proposals and suggestions,[11] which have become

---

[11] See *Official Records of the General Assembly, Tenth Special Session, Plenary Meetings*, 1st to 25th meetings; *ibid., Tenth Special Session, Supplement No. 1* (A/S-10/1), *Supplement No. 2* (A/S-10/2 and Corr.1), *Supplement No. 2A* (A/S-10/2/Add.1/Rev.1) and *Supplement No. 3* (A/S-10/3 and Corr.1); *ibid., Tenth Special Session, Annexes*, agenda item 7, document A/S-10/10; and *ibid., Tenth Special*

an integral part of the work of the special session of the General Assembly, deserve to be studied further and more thoroughly, taking into consideration the many relevant comments and observations made in both the general debate in plenary meeting and the deliberations of the *Ad Hoc* Committee of the Tenth Special Session, the Secretary-General is requested to transmit, together with this Final Document, to the appropriate deliberative and negotiating organs dealing with the questions of disarmament all the official records of the special session devoted to disarmament, in accordance with the recommendations which the Assembly may adopt at its thirty-third session. Some of the proposals put forth for the consideration of the special session are listed below:

(a) Text of the decision of the Central Committee of the Romanian Communist Party concerning Romania's position on disarmament and, in particular, on nuclear disarmament, adopted on 9 May 1978;[12]

(b) Views of the Swiss Government on problems to be discussed at the tenth special session of the General Assembly;[13]

(c) Proposals of the Union of Soviet Socialist Republics on practical measures for ending the arms race;[14]

(d) Memorandum from France concerning the establishment of an International Satellite Monitoring Agency;[15]

Session, Ad Hoc *Committee of the Tenth Special Session,* 1st to 16th meetings, and *ibid.,* Ad Hoc *Committee of the Tenth Special Session, Sessional Fascicle,* corrigendum; A/S-10/5, A/S-10/6 and Corr.1 and Add.1, A/S-10/7 and Corr.1, A/S-10/8 and Add.1 and 2, A/S-10/9, A/S-10/11-14 and A/S-10/17; A/S-10/AC.1/1-8, A/S-10/AC.1/9 and Add.1, A/S-10/AC.1/10 and 11, A/S-10/AC.1/12 and Corr.1, A/S-10/AC.1/13-25, A/S-10/AC.1/26 and Corr.1 and 2, A/S-10/AC.1/27-26, A/S-10/AC.1/37 and Rev.1 and Corr.1 and Rev.1/Add.1, and A/S-10/AC.1/38-40; A/S-10/AC.1/L.1 and Rev.1 and A/S-10/AC.1/L.2-17.
[12] A/S-10/14.
[13] A/S-10/AC.1/2.
[14] A/S-10/AC.1/4.
[15] A/S-10/AC.1/7.

(e) Memorandum from France concerning the establishment of an International Institute for Research on Disarmament;[16]

(f) Proposal by Sri Lanka for the establishment of a World Disarmament Authority;[17]

(g) Working paper submitted by the Federal Republic of Germany entitled "Contribution to the seismological verification of a comprehensive test ban";[18]

(h) Working paper submitted by the Federal Republic of Germany entitled "Invitation to attend an international chemical-weapon verification workshop in the Federal Republic of Germany";[19]

(i) Working paper submitted by China on disarmament;[20]

(j) Working paper submitted by the Federal Republic of Germany concerning zones of confidence-building measures as a first step towards the preparation of the world-wide convention on confidence-building measures;[21]

(k) Proposal by Ireland for a study of the possibility of establishing a system of incentives to promote arms control and disarmament;[22]

(l) Working paper submitted by Romania concerning a synthesis of the proposals in the field of disarmament;[23]

(m) Proposal by the United States of America on the establishment of a United Nations Peace-keeping Reserve and on confidence-building measures and stabilizing measures in various regions, including notification of manoeuvres, invitation of

---

[16] A/S-10/AC.1/8.
[17] A/S-10/AC.1/9 and Add.1.
[18] A/S-10/AC.1/12 and Corr.1.
[19] A/S-10/AC.1/13.
[20] A/S-10/AC.1/17.
[21] A/S-10/AC.1/20.
[22] A/S-10/AC.1/21.
[23] A/S-10/AC.1/23.

observers to manoeuvres, and United Nations machinery to study and promote such measures;[24]

(n)   Proposal by Uruguay on the possibility of establishing a polemological agency;[25]

(o)   Proposal by Belgium, Canada, Denmark, Germany, Federal Republic of, Ireland, Italy, Japan, Luxembourg, the Netherlands, New Zealand, Norway, Sweden, the United Kingdom of Great Britain and Northern Ireland and the United States of America on the strengthening of the security role of the United Nations in the peaceful settlement of disputes and peace-keeping;[26]

(p)   Memorandum   from   France   concerning   the establishment   of   an   International   Disarmament   Fund   for Development;[27]

(q)   Proposal by Norway entitled "Evaluation of the impact of new weapons on arms control and disarmament efforts";[28]

(r)   Note verbale transmitting the text, signed in Washington on 22 June 1978 by the Ministers for Foreign Affairs of Argentina, Bolivia, Chile, Colombia, Ecuador, Panama, Peru and Venezuela, reaffirming the principles of the Declaration of Ayacucho with respect to the limitation of conventional weapons;[29]

(s)   Memorandum from Liberia entitled "Declaration of a new philosophy on disarmament";[30]

(t)   Statements made by the representatives of China, on 22 June 1978, on the draft Final Document of the tenth special session;[31]

---

[24] A/S-10/AC.1/24.
[25] A/S-10/AC.1/25.
[26] A/S-10/AC.1/26 and Corr.1 and 2.
[27] A/S-10/AC.1/28.
[28] A/S-10/AC.1/31.
[29] A/S-10/AC.1/34.
[30] A/S-10/AC.1/35.
[31] A/S-10/AC.1/36.

(u)   Proposal by the President of Cyprus for the total demilitarization and disarmament of the Republic of Cyprus and the implementation of the resolutions of the United Nations;[32]

(v)   Proposal by Costa Rica on economic and social incentives to halt the arms race;[33]

(w)   Amendments submitted by China to the draft Final Document of the tenth special session;[34]

(x)   Proposals by Canada for the implementation of a strategy of suffocation of the nuclear arms race;[35]

(y)   Draft resolution submitted by Cyprus, Ethiopia and India on the urgent need for cessation of further testing of nuclear weapons;[36]

(z)   Draft resolution submitted by Ethiopia and India on the non-use of nuclear weapons and prevention of nuclear war;[37]

(aa)   Proposal by the non-aligned countries on the establishment of a zone of peace in the Mediterranean;[38]

(bb)   Proposal by the Government of Senegal for a tax on military budgets;[39]

(cc)   Proposal by Austria for the transmission to Member States of working paper A/AC.187/109 and the ascertainment of their views on the subject of verification;[40]

(dd)   Proposal by the non-aligned countries for the dismantling of foreign military bases in foreign territories and withdrawal of foreign troops from foreign territories;[41]

---

[32] A/S-10/AC.1/39.
[33] A/S-10/AC.1/40.
[34] A/S-10/AC.1/L.2-4, A/S-10/AC.1/L.7 and 8.
[35] A/S-10/AC.1/L.6.
[36] A/S-10/AC.1/L.10.
[37] A/S-10/AC.1/L.11.
[38] A/S-10/AC.1/37, para. 72.
[39] Ibid., para. 101.
[40] Ibid., para. 113.
[41] Ibid., para. 126.

(ee)   Proposal by Mexico for the opening, on a provisional basis, of an *ad hoc* account in the United Nations Development Programme to use for development the funds which may be released as a result of disarmament measures;[42]

(ff)   Proposal by Italy on the role of the Security Council in the field of disarmament in accordance with Article 26 of the Charter of the United Nations;[43]

(gg) Proposal by the Netherlands for a study on the establishment of an international disarmament organization.[44]

126. In adopting this Final Document, the States Members of the United Nations solemnly reaffirm their determination to work for general and complete disarmament and to make further collective efforts aimed at strengthening peace and international security; eliminating the threat of war, particularly nuclear war; implementing practical measures aimed at halting and reversing the arms race; strengthening the procedures for the peaceful settlement of disputes; and reducing military expenditures and utilizing the resources thus released in a manner which will help to promote the well-being of all peoples and to improve the economic conditions of the developing countries.

127. The General Assembly expresses its satisfaction that the proposals submitted to its special session devoted to disarmament and the deliberations thereon have made it possible to reaffirm and define in this Final Document fundamental principles, goals, priorities and procedures for the implementation of the above purposes, either in the Declaration or the Programme of Action or in both. The Assembly also welcomes the important decisions agreed upon regarding the deliberative and negotiating machinery and is confident that these organs will discharge their functions in an effective manner.

128. Finally, it should be borne in mind that the number of States that participated in the general debate, as well as the high level of representation and the depth and scope of that debate,

---

[42]   Ibid., para. 141.
[43]   Ibid., para. 179.
[44]   Ibid., para. 186.

are unprecedented in the history of disarmament efforts. Several Heads of State or Government addressed the General Assembly. In addition, other Heads of State or Government sent messages and expressed their good wishes for the success of the special session of the Assembly. Several high officials of specialized agencies and other institutions and programmes within the United Nations system and spokesmen of twenty-five non-governmental organizations and six research institutes also made valuable contributions to the proceedings of the session. It must be emphasized, moreover, that the special session marks not the end but rather the beginning of a new phase of the efforts of the United Nations in the field of disarmament.

129. The General Assembly is convinced that the discussions of the disarmament problems at the special session and its Final Document will attract the attention of all peoples, further mobilize world public opinion and provide a powerful impetus for the cause of disarmament.

27th plenary meeting
30 June 1978

*

* *

The President of the General Assembly subsequently informed the Secretary-General[45] that the Committee on Disarmament, referred to in paragraph 120 of the above resolution, would be open to the nuclear-weapon States and to the following thirty-five States: ALGERIA, ARGENTINA, AUSTRALIA, BELGIUM, BRAZIL, BULGARIA, BURMA, CANADA, CUBA, CZECHOSLOVAKIA, EGYPT, ETHIOPIA, GERMAN DEMOCRATIC REPUBLIC, GERMANY, FEDERAL REPUBLIC OF, HUNGARY, INDIA, INDONESIA, IRAN, ITALY, JAPAN, KENYA, MEXICO, MONGOLIA, MOROCCO, NETHERLANDS, NIGERIA, PAKISTAN, PERU, POLAND, ROMANIA, SRI LANKA, SWEDEN, VENEZUELA, YUGOSLAVIA AND ZAIRE.

---

[45] A/S-10/24.

www.ingramcontent.com/pod-product-compliance
Lightning Source LLC
Chambersburg PA
CBHW052126090426

42741CB00009B/1966